THE SOCIETY OF CLASSICAL POETS

JOURNAL X

Mantyk · Anderson · Grein · Magdalen

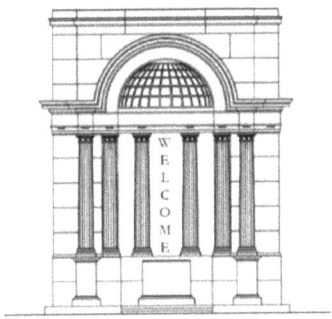

Classical Poets Publishing

———

Mount Hope, New York

Editors: Evan Mantyk (Lead), C.B. Anderson (Selections and Copyediting), Dusty Grein (Layout), Daniel Magdalen (Art)

All poems granted permission by poets and previously published on the Society of Classical Poets' website ClassicalPoets.org between February 1, 2021, and January 31, 2022

All poets retain rights over their individual poems.

All contemporary artwork used with permission of the artist. Other artworks are in the public domain.

Cover Art Front: *Magnificent Outpouring* by Laura Westlake

Cover Art Back: *Poetry* by Paul Erlandson

"The Society of Classical Poets Edifice" on title page by Michael Curtis

Image on page 34: *The Three Fates Clotho, Lachesis, and Atropos* by Giorgio Ghisi, 1558–59, on engraving, 5.42 x 8.74 in.

Inquiries and Membership: submissions@classicalpoets.org

ISBN: 978-1-949398-66-3

Copyright © 2022 by The Society of Classical Poets, Inc.
ALL RIGHTS RESERVED

Contents

Introduction	5
I. The Muse's Song	9
II. Love Poems	83
III. Humor	97
IV. China	149
V. The West	165
VI. Narratives	193
VII. Translations	219
VIII. Essays	259
Poet Biographies	293

INTRODUCTION

This year marks the tenth year since the founding of the Society of Classical Poets in the office of *The Epoch Times* newspaper in July 2012. Coinciding with this milestone, the Journal you now hold in your hands is the Society's tenth such journal and earlier this year we concluded the Society's tenth annual international poetry competition—which is now, as far as I can tell, the largest and most significant general poetry contest dedicated to purely traditional English poetry.

In a decade, the Society has grown tremendously thanks to the efforts of many exceptional poets, readers, patrons, commenters, editors, and staff. They have made the Society a very dynamic and creative place to keep coming back to, featuring a splendid array of new poems every day; insightful comments, essays, and reviews that enrich the minds of readers; poetry contests and challenges that push poets in unexpected and exciting ways; and poetry readings that have added an extra level of depth and reality to the entire experience.

Every year, we try to do exactly what we did the previous year, but better, in some cases introducing things that work and stopping others that didn't, evolving and perfecting everything year to year. Your feedback is welcome if you ever have a new idea or thoughts you feel the Society may benefit from. Such feedback can be sent through the usual channel to the submissions email address.

Changes can also be found in this year's Journal. This year, the sections have been somewhat streamlined. The first section "The Muse's Song" is meant to simply be the main section for poetry in general, merging what we have in previous years called "In Admiration" (or "Beauty" some years) and "Observations." All of the other sections are more narrowly focused on a particular subject area or style.

Additionally, this year we have added more essays. First, there is a dagger-like essay, short and sharp, from Dr. Joseph S. Salemi that points to five common rules for poetry writers as well as five uncommon rules, and, perhaps most importantly, an overarching guiding principle on how to view them all. Dr. Salemi has done a great service to poets today in writing this and I highly recommend reading it.

Next, there is a review by James Sale of the first volume (maybe the only?) of Andrew Benson Brown's epic, *Legends of Liberty*. America does not have a truly successful epic poem of its own, and Benson Brown may very well have done it—though Time will have to be the ultimate judge. At any rate, he has created a work filled with action, history, and a vision that is exciting and indeed epic. Some of my favorite lines come from the poem's very first stanza. They tie so well together the ancient tradition of the epic, its state of neglect today, and the underlying social problems we face today:

> Our age has lost all its affinity
> For epic tales of toxic masculinity.

Reviewer Sale shares some of his favorites as well. As someone who has taught American history before, I can say without a doubt that excerpts of Benson Brown's poem, if not this entire volume, would be ideal for breathing passion and creativity, in a positive and constructive way, into stifled high school and college classrooms.

Next, Adam Sedia's in-depth essay examines solipsism in English poetry today, revealing its restricted and vapid nature, its 19th century origin, and finally its antidote. Solipsism, according to Merriam Webster, is "a theory holding that the self can know nothing but its own modifications and that the self is the only existent thing"—basically it means extreme selfishness and self-absorption. The essay's methodical nature works to effectively lay bare a key problem with poetry today and its solution.

As an addendum to Sedia's essay, I add that it is a generally accepted truth among poets and the poetry establishment today that more people in the English-speaking world should appreciate and recognize poetry. The way to bring about such appreciation and recognition is to restore a format, a definition of poetry, that people naturally recognize, meaning the restoration of meter and rhyme. Those on the right side of poetry's history, who are illuminated in Sedia's essay, used meter and rhyme; and those lost in the murky puddle of solipsism used meter and rhyme little or not at all. To put it another way, it is self-absorbed and counter-productive to begin with your own definition of what constitutes a poem regardless of the basic sense of it that most people innately have and regardless of the traditional conventions handed down by millennia of poets in Western and even Eastern civilizations. I am reminded of when I interviewed the prominent poet A.M. Juster last year. He said: "Big Poetry would deny that the move away from formal verse caused the decline of public interest in and support for poetry, but the evidence overwhelmingly contradicts that view." I wholeheartedly agree with Juster.

Next, a special thank-you to poet and artist Paul Erlandson for creating the first original painting specifically for an SCP Journal. It can be seen on the back cover of this Journal as well as inside. My take on it is that the allegorical figures represent readers today drawing inspiration from traditional poetry. Some draw a sense of delightful beauty that helps them to continue singing sweetly, so to speak, while others take heart in the order and intricacy, which helps them to continue the day-to-day battle of life with a sense of purpose. The fountain in the background perhaps represents poetry as part of the fountainhead of civilization. Indeed, poetry is found near the heart of most cultures and civilizations. Erlandson's cross pollination of arts with classical poetry is something I hope to see more of in the future. Already, Jack DesBois and James A. Tweedie have done splendid work in combining classical poetry and music.

Finally, I'll end with a reason to love poetry. This comes from a poetry challenge initiated by poet Roy E. Peterson, who invited poets to take a famous quote about poetry and turn the quote itself into poetry. Susan Jarvis Bryant, the Lady of Prodigious Poetry herself, took a quote from 19th century writer Robert Louis Stevenson, "Wine is bottled poetry," and, diverging somewhat I think from Stevenson's meaning, wrote something nonetheless brilliant, which I will end with:

> I pick words from the grapevine—plump and sweet,
> Then roll their ripened wonder round my tongue;
> Extract their potent essence till they greet
> My senses with intoxicating fun.

—Evan Mantyk, March 2022

I. THE MUSE'S SONG

Mt. Washington in Autumn by Erik Koeppel, 2019, oil on panel, 18 x 15 in. (www.erikkoeppel.com)

Autumn

by Joe Tessitore

You'll notice, 'round this time of year,
That to the flowers they hold dear,
The bees will cling the whole night through—
And if you loved them, wouldn't you?

So what if evening's deadly chill
May be the final, bitter pill
That brings your life unto its end—
Where else would you these moments spend?

And if it's not your time, just yet,
Praise ye the Lord and may He let
The rising sun do what it does …
And 'round your favorite flowers buzz.

An Autumn Path

by Angel L. Villanueva

The path he takes this early day
Is dressed in dew and straws of hay.
The morning mist obscures his view;
The barn, though near, seems far away.

The sleepy sun begins to rise,
And light prepares to climb the skies.
He sees the path much clearer now,
As life awakened fills his eyes.

He senses changes autumn brings,
A mix of scents from lovely things.
The air, perfumed by turning leaves,
Is fragrance loved by serfs and kings.

Above he hears migrating birds,
Their calls of joy, like soothing words.
They tell of lands where warmth awaits:
A transient home for flocks and herds.

The cows have stirred and move about,
And roosters crow as piglets rout.
A dog begins to run to him,
His faithful friend and eager scout.

So much to do while autumn stays,
Before the freeze of winter's gaze.
And yet, for now, he walks the path,
And sings a psalm of morning praise.

The Lovely World

by Martin Rizley

Behold the frozen, flaxen fields at morn—
The tall grass shining on the hills of clay
Which sunlit wisps of winter frost adorn
In dazzling white, as for a bridal day.

An air of holy wantonness imbues
The outspread earth which, quiet as a nun,
Displays her swelling curves and ardent hues,
A naked lover to the rising sun.

Like golden apples gathered in a cart
Or honey stored for winter in a hive,
I store up these sweet moments in my heart,
And think, "How grand it is to be alive!"

When suddenly, a spasm of the mind,
A shooting pang, now cramps my stretching soul;
For I must die one day and leave behind
This lovely world for deeps beyond life's shoal!

Someday, just like these fields before me now,
I, too, must lie enshrouded, for the same
Cold, icy hand of death will brush my brow
And draw a pall of white over my frame.

Like one who climbs a rugged mount and slips,
I, too, shall slip while striving to ascend
Life's final slope, and though my fingertips
Strain bravely, they shall slacken in the end.

At once, a gloomy shadow veils my heart:
I find myself upon a barren plain,
The world's negative, its counterpart,
Where pain and sorrow, wrath and terror reign.

That dreaded scene of loneliness where plagues,
Disasters, famines, wars, and dark despair
Have drunk the blood of thousands to the dregs,
Whose blind, ill-fated steps had led them there.

Yet, from that dreadful place, I see unfurled
More clearly from afar, the world I love;
Behold! It is the image of a world
Whose beams of glory stream down from above!

A world that beckons hope to build upon
More solid ground than can be found below,
A world of endless light, eternal dawn,
Whose joy no shade of death can overthrow!

A Winter in Uzbekistan

by Peter Hartley

A winter in Uzbekistan so cold
And raw and brittle, on the steppes some years
Ago, the day we saw three dogs whose ears
Had crudely been cut off, so we were told,
To render them more docile, more controlled.
It kept their livestock safe, quelled farmers' fears;
An outrage to their natures it appears,
To maim those dogs to bar their being bold.

And then we noticed one of them had lost
A leg. His kennel-mate would lean daylong
Against him, keep him upright in the frost:
In such a manner both would get along.
Compassion surely taught one to assist
As surely trust helped both to coexist.

The Joys of Spring

a pantoum

by Janice Canerdy

It's here—sweet long-awaited spring.
New blooms smell lovely; skies are blue.
The trilling birds are on the wing.
Earth has awakened; life is new.

New blooms smell lovely; skies are blue.
Kids dash outside to have a fling.
Earth has awakened; life is new.
This time exudes a unique zing.

Kids dash outside to have a fling.
The joys of spring seem overdue.
This time exudes a unique zing.
Who could resist the springtime view?

The joys of spring seem overdue
for those who love what warm days bring.
Who could resist a springtime view
when not just birds but people sing?

For those who love what warm days bring,
the trilling birds are on the wing
when not just birds but people sing.
It's here—sweet long-awaited spring.

An Asian Courtyard by Fei Meng, 2020, painted in Photoshop with Wacom pen & tablet. (www.feimengart.com)

Plum Blossom Blessings

by Margaret Coats

The pine, bamboo, and plum are winter's friends,
Yet plum trees bloom to overcome the chill
And herald spring. Resilient health extends
Throughout my struggling mind and body ill;
Spiced fragrance with that ruby beauty blends.

Flame-draped in cozy apricot orange twill,
A wealth of blossoms spills straight from the bough,
Enriching me with comforts that fulfill
My needs, and promise richly to endow
My home and friends with goods I give at will.

Touching a silvered branch, I wonder how
Twelve pearly moons may benefit this year;
Full ripened virtue is my glowing vow,
Allegiance to the radiance I revere
With strength these growing snow white buds show now.

Longevity like velvet wields a spear
That's tipped with force, but smoothly helps me dare
Oppose time's ravages through murrey cheer,
An atmosphere advancing wisdom's flair
As customary music flowers here.

Its wintersweet ambrosial thoroughfare
A happy death and renaissance portends;
For peaceful silence, plum's the word to air:
New bathed in rosy myrrh, the soul ascends
When years begin with pink bouquets of prayer.

MURREY: Purplish black, mulberry colored.
POET'S NOTE: In Chinese lore, the five-petaled plum blossom represents the five blessings of health, wealth, virtue, longevity, and a calm, happy death. The longevity stanza above alludes to the plum blossom spear, a "king of weapons" in martial arts, well suited to agile elders.

I Asked the Moon

by David Irby

I asked the moon, "Do you feel all alone?"
She said, "I have no time. I've lots to do.
To all the stars, I am a chaperone.
Tonight I'm in good company with you."

I asked the moon, "Do you begrudge the sun?"
She said, "my heart's devoid of jealousy.
Besides the job I do could not be done
without the nightly light she lends to me."

I asked the moon, "Why shine upon my face,
when I feel so unworthy of your glow?"
She said, "my child, you're worthy of my grace
like every other form of life below."

I said, "you are so beautiful, my friend.
How does it feel to rule nocturnal skies?"
She said "I do not rule. I just attend
to everything from stars to fireflies.

"I am no queen. I'm only meant to serve
and keep the void of darkness well at bay.
My purpose here is mostly to observe
and keep you safe until the break of day."

I smiled then bid the moon a fond goodnight
and thanked her for the haven of her beams.
Then in a cloud, she vanished from my sight,
but on the wind I heard her say "Sweet dreams."

With How Sad Steps

from a Philip Sidney sonnet

by Peter Austin

With how sad steps, O Moon, you climb the skies!
How silently, and with how wan a face!
What see you? Humankind's excessive pace
Getting from here to there? We are not wise,
Who to alarm clock daily need arise,
At nighttime weary steps to bed retrace
Half drunk, the day's displeasures to erase
And lie there, in the dark, with unshut eyes.

For what, so mad a gallop to the wire?
Retirement: frail, dyspeptic *mals vivants*,
Damning the crossword, dozing by the fire,
Scanning the news with mordant nonchalance,
Shaking off the temptation to inquire,
Did we slow down to smell the roses once?'

Night Verses

by Brian Palmer

The airy rush of thoughts today
The evening breeze has whisked away.

The wind that spoke to me in wings
Has flown and left old, scattered things.

Some small and faint discarded words
Remain like fragile bones of birds.

I gather letters from the ground,
Recall their lofty flight and sound.

I turn their verses rune by rune
To lines beneath the harvest moon.

Revived, deciphered bird I know
I'll hold a moment, then let go.

Owl Ensconced on Oaken Branch

by Corey Elizabeth Jackson

Owl ensconced on oaken branch,
   A wingèd spirit rare,
His gaze is wisdom: calm, intent,
   Bewitching and aware.

Soulful and implacable,
   His feathered stillness bright
Is outlined by cerulean sky,
   A beacon of the night.

Behind stark owl a full moon glows,
   Casts vectored rays of light,
And yon in inky distance pierce
   Sweet stars his friends in flight.

But tawny owl remains transfixed
   Upon his earthly tree,
Before he soars in darkest realm,
   Sage spirit flying free.

Carolina Wren, photo by Susan Jarvis Bryant, 2021.

Ode to Hidden Splendor

by Susan Jarvis Bryant

I heard your rolling croon beyond my vision
Blooming in the balm of winter's breeze—
A thrilling spill of crystalline precision
Amid the Spanish moss draped on the trees.
My heart took flight with each falsetto note,
Then fluttered at the height of your refrains—
The dazzle and pizzazz of soaring song
Rising from your silken-feathered throat.
Your air, beyond compare on coastal plains,
Resounded with a twang so sweet and strong.
Yet when I looked above for lemon wings
With cobalt tints and glints of scarlet down
(A rainbow-garbed soprano trilling hymns)
My eyes fell on your form of dusty brown.
All set to spy a diva of the sky,
I reeled and gasped in wonder and surprise.
Oh, Carolina Wren I must declare,
I would have passed your majesty right by
Had I not seen you sing with my own eyes,
Oh, shy and tiny gem extraordinaire!

And now I scan the shadows for a pearl.
I comb drab corners for a golden ray.
I watch the buds and butterflies unfurl
And hunt for silver in the greyest day.
I walk the darkest paths among the ferns,
Where cobwebs decked with diamonds lace the verge,
And armadillos doze till dawn of night.
I relish misty routes of twists and turns,
Remembering your lush, symphonious surge
That dipped your hidden splendor in the light.

Haiku

Fog enshrouds the night
Woven in the heavy mist
A thread of fireflies

—Joe Tessitore

Spring in the hedgerows
Magpies busy canceling
Fresh twitter accounts

—Sean Hickey

How short is freedom
gained by the cherry blossom
released from the branch

—Germain Droogenbroodt

Bear cubs watching men
Walking through a sylvan glen
The forest shudders

—Roy E. Peterson

The young boy splashes
in the backyard swimming pool
facing subs and sharks

—Bruce Dale Wise

Falling August stars
The sky is full of beauty
So many wishes

—Vita

A minute's silence
for the atomic bomb day
The wind also dies

原爆忌風も静かに黙祷す

   —Toshiji Kawagoe

        end of the summer—
        the calm surface of a lake
        absorbs the twilight

          —Marek Kozubek

Curious concert—
crickets croon to a cornfield
of indifferent ears

   —Martin Elster

        taste of morning tea
        the delicate ray of sun
        through an icicle

          —Daniela Misso

Dark branches stripped bare
cold and sad, quite unaware
stirrings down below

   —Linette Eloff

NOTE: The above haiku were the winner and runners-up of the Society of Classical Poets 2021 Haiku Competition, Judged by Margaret Coats

The Magpie's Chorus

by David Watt

With sunlight at full power
And silence in the air,
I sought a shaded bower,
A cool drink, and a chair.
But then, I heard the trilling
Of magpies in the trees
Pour out like liquid filling
The desiccated breeze.

They put on airs and graces,
In obvious delight
At raising piebald faces
To launch their song in flight;
And in the process, showing
That sound waves travel best
Through spaces brightly glowing
From summer's heat expressed.

I hear their sweet song often
In seasons less intense;
But when their trebles soften
I lose the inner sense
That all the world is listening
With boundless gratitude
To notes so pure they're glistening
On peaks of amplitude.

Give me the magpie's chorus
When summer's at its height;
Their lilting song calls for us
To linger in that light
Which some may find oppressive,
Or blinding to the eye—
To thrill at trills impressive,
And lift our spirits high.

Perfect Apples

by C.B. Anderson

The Law of Perfect Apples says it all:
A malic acid tang pervades the crisp
And shocking mouth appeal that tells you fall
Is under way. If you should catch a wisp

Of summer turning winter in the play
Your tongue and nose were first created for,
You'll later fondly recollect the day
When autumn's dearest gift unhinged the door

That barred you from the vertigo your heart
Decided on as reason tried to keep
The bliss at bay. There isn't any chart
To guide you through the future. Go to sleep,

And let the maze of hazy hours stem
The tendency to parse and analyze.
Forget the waning sun: no requiem
Is called for to observe the light's demise,

For seasons come and go, and come again.
Enjoy the fruit, now plentiful and sweet;
Remember that the Sabbath is for men
And not for gods; make plans to overeat.

Farmer,

by C.B. Anderson

Unpack the dormant forces quiet days
Have put aside and stoke the smothered fire
Whose soot fanned out in lifeless carbon rays
Upon the hearth of winter's mild repose,
But bear the fire within—long days require
A bolder stroke. The spring comes to a close,
And summer spawns a host from hell's own choir:
The heat, the blistered dawns, the gnash of hoes.
Though all the pressing needs were ably met
From solstice to the fall, do not repair
Too quickly to the lavish table set
For hero's welcome. Many things remain
Undone: the harvest of next winter's fare,
The nurture owed the very kind terrain
That fosters life, the praise of freshened air
And all-sustaining sun, and prayers for rain.

My Mother's Eyes

by Carl Kinsky

We took a ride into the countryside
to search for bluebells but we first saw phlox.
Delighted by the sight my mother cried,
"Look at the flowers flutter on the rocks!
Look at the bluebells!" I looked at my clock.
Long ride, no blue, no bells, but don't be snide.
Still I replied, "They're flirts like new spring frocks,
But they're not bluebells. Bluebells are spring's pride
and joy, much better than phlox." I can't hide
my thoughts so well, but I tried not to mock
her as she saw by the creek, eyes sky wide,
parades of bluebells, face rapt and awestruck.

I wish I could see with my mother's eyes
bluebells and phlox, perpetually surprised.

Birds in Flight

by David Whippman

"Free as a bird," that's what we always say,
"It's time to spread my wings and fly away,
I have to find myself, fly high and free!"
Birds are the metaphors of liberty.
They seem free, for they have the gift of flight,
to move in three dimensions as they might,
gliding untrammeled: all the classic scenes
in paintings, poems and the movie screens!
The seascapes where they soar with mournful cries
over the ocean, in the open skies.
It isn't really so: their path is mapped
and predetermined; instinct has them trapped.
Just like remote control, some unseen force
will keep them moving on just one set course.
Aren't we the same? We head back to a nest,
To boundaries that someone else deems best.
We cannot think for long outside the box;
we move with others in conforming flocks.

Birds in Flight

by Evan Mantyk

A bird's heart beats about ten times the speed
Of man's. He reads the signs that supersede
What we perceive; he can predict a storm,
Presage an earthquake's shocks, and as a norm
Can navigate without a GPS.
And in old myths? A bird can curse or bless.
Two eagles' flight foretells the *Odyssey*
Is near its end and one day faithfully
The hero will bring long due punishment.
In ancient China, phoenix sightings meant
A sage was born on Earth, a golden age
Had come. A bird may fit within a cage
Indeed, but on the clouds his spirit flies.
Though one may sink, ten thousand more will rise
Connected by the innate traits of race
Into a single mind transcending space.
And thus they can deliver omens' news,
Which share so freely with us Heaven's views.

Lotus Hand, sculpture by Johanna Schwaiger, 2021.
(johannaschwaiger.com)

The Blacksmith God Forges Scenes on Achilles' Shield

after Homer's Iliad *Book 18*

by Evan Mantyk

The hammer strikes! And glowing sparks fly out
As Earth takes shape and then the flowing seas,
The sun, the moon, the wondrous Pleiades
And all the constellations round about.

The hammer strikes! And now the god makes cities,
Also countryside where joy and sadness
Battle back and forth: war's bloody madness
Here and there a farmer sings sweet ditties.

Then crowning all of man's experience,
He forges dance—the gracefulness and skill
Of matching inner art with muscles' will
To spin and leap with poised exuberance.

This gem of civilization now in place,
His gift is taken to the human race.

Three Sisters

by Cheryl Corey

Clotho

When mother sat me down, I feared the worst.
Her words, however, offered praise instead.
"Your gentle hands are motherly," she said.
"That's why I've chosen you to be the first
of three, the Fates, henceforth to spin the thread
of life." I sit before the spinning wheel,
and every thread I spin, I spin with zeal,
to make my mother proud. The sheep are led
to shearing, wool is carded, washed. I feel
the texture, baby-soft; and then there's silk
from spun cocoons (to me that's mother's milk).
I hold a world within my hands, reveal
the birthing child as either girl or boy,
and every thread's a life that brings me joy.

Lachesis

We sisters three, the Fates, as progeny
of Themis, she who counsels Jove, are bound
by laws of gods, not men. "Your mind is sound,
your instinct good. Responsibility
is yours to render judgment as to death;
and notwithstanding every life's a treasure,
as Clotho spins, so you will take the measure,
the moment they will draw their final breath."
My mother's words were like a smithy's weight,
but inner strength was always my cuirass.
My oath: to meet and hopefully surpass
all expectation, prove there's more to Fate
than happenstance; and so, as law demands,
I hold a thread of life between my hands.

Atropos

I cut the thread of life as Lachesis
commands, yet I'm the sister hated most;
while Clotho, always pale, is like a ghost,
but plays a sweetheart role, our darling sis.
I often feel that mine's a thankless job.
It calls for perfect vision, nerves of steel,
and steady hands. No matter what I feel,
I mustn't let them see or hear me sob.
Instead, I focus on the tools of trade:
my newest toy, a laser, cleanly cuts,
but if I'm off a hair, I get tut-tuts.
I also have a special scalpel, made
of black obsidian found on isles of Greece.
To all the lives I end—rest in peace.

Back to The Beginning

"I want answers. I want all the words the poem whispers to be made flesh, to sit opposite me, and to shout out the reason for our existence…"
—*Susan Jarvis Bryant on Daniel Kemper's "An Intelligent Cup of Coffee"*

by Mike Bryant

He who is, and always was, spoke light
And made our tiny place. That light, His clay,
He fashioned into width and depth and height,
And earth and water, us, and night and day.

And every part of every thing; of space
And flesh and stars and time, are all the same—
A single thing—His words pronounced with grace.
And He, I Am, calls out to all by name.

Whatever was and is must answer Him
By being just what they were made to be.
No, we were not created on a whim,
But in His image, and by His decree.

Creation He's bequeathed to every voice.
Our words can build or raze, can curse or praise,
And every utterance is by our choice—
To mutter sheepishly or else to blaze.

Magnificat

by Brian Yapko

Praise Him for the lightning in the gale,
For balmy winds, for crystals in the snow.
Wonder at the gaudy peacock's tail,
Observe how huge the elephant can grow!

The turtledove, the maculate giraffe,
The leopard's feral stealth, the eagle's wing,
The neighing of the horse, the dolphin's laugh;
The joy in God which once made Mary sing.

Praise God for all the miracles to be!
The enemy who may become a friend;
The captive who yearns one day to be free;
The woes of life we all hope to transcend.

Praise God for each new morning that we greet!
And praise Him for creation left undone.
God's work is left for humans to complete
To follow in the footsteps of His Son.

We all are burdened by life's heavy chain
And wearied by this broken road we trod.
But as I live I will not bow to pain.
My soul sings the magnificence of God!

Aristotle with a Bust of Homer by Rembrandt Harmenszoon van Rijn, 1653, oil on canvas, 56.39 x 53.70 in.

Contemplating Aristotle Contemplating a Bust of Homer

by James A. Tweedie

He stands enwrapped in luminous shadowed light,
A woven cord of gold across his chest,
Voluminous silk sleeves of purest white
Contrast the deep-black velvet of his vest.
Arrayed as though he were a wealthy man;
A citizen of Rembrandt's Amsterdam.

An Aristotle lost in time and space;
The Netherlands reborn as ancient Greece;
The past as present, brush-stroked into place,
An artist's metaphoric masterpiece.
As time stands still, the sage's eyes embrace
The enigmatic, stone-blind Homer's face.

The famed philosopher and polymath
Of all that is and was and yet shall be,
Now walks his thoughts down a mimetic path
That leads to music, art and poetry,
And lays his hand of blessing on the head
Of one whose words yet live though he be dead.

Like Aristotle we look to the past,
And see Achilles on the fields of Troy.
And from that tragic tale return at last
To home, a wife's long-suffering love, and joy.
We place the bust of Homer on our shelves
And deem him greater than we deem ourselves.

Civis Romanus Sum

(I am a Roman citizen)

by Alex Rubstein, high school poet

As Paul stood bound and for the whip outstretched,
He said to the centurion beside,
"'Tis lawful here for you to flog a wretch,
A Roman citizen and not yet tried?"

The mere centurion on hearing went
And to the tribune swiftly said, "Take heed!
What art thou 'bout to do? What foul intent!
This man, a Roman citizen, doth plead!"

Ere Rome's decline, one treasure, *civitas*,
The whip could stay, all civil rights obtain,
And fill Paul's captors with such grave distress
For having put a citizen in chains.

To reap respect, and envy, civil bloom,
One merely said, *Civis Romanus sum*.

The Soldier Keeps the Wolf at Bay

by Roy E. Peterson

The soldier keeps the wolf at bay
So we may never see it.
That is why the young today
Simply don't believe it.

You say "We see no wolf out there?
So why should we believe you?"
The wolf is hiding in his lair
The better to deceive you.

And as the light grows dimmer then
The wolf will come to prey
So hold fast to those fighting men
Who keep the wolf at bay.

Sir Percival

by Alan Grant

A quiet desperation lives within
my soul: to find the Holy Cup, the Grail;
to touch something beyond this mortal pen,
and taste my God, His blood, from Cross's nail.

I am not worthy, this I know too well,
though we are all the Son, all Christ, or could
be Him if we'd but try abjuring Hell—
but Hell grows deep within like poisoned wood—

yet am I least of those I call "brother",
not half so great as good Sir Galahad,
nor stalwart nor as strong as bold Sir Bors,
nor courteous like Gawain, humble lad,

nor skilled as cursed Sir Lancelot with sword,
but yet in me a passion burns: longing
to know my Maker, hear His flesh made Word,
that like un-quenching flame peels back my skin

revealing such deep pits within they ring
with sound—shrill screams, and trumpets loud,
as though angelic hosts and Satan's throng
clash in the firmament—while I am bound,

tethered to flesh and failure, one lost name,
that yet will not forsake this quest, to yearn
and strive with all my aching heart—in pain
that close resembles ecstasy—and learn,

at last, what one droplet of Christ's dark blood
could purge from this vessel of clay and bone;
at last, the meaning, all—completely understood,
in one pure instant revelation known:

why I was perfectly imperfect made,
and all my destiny, so long concealed,
would be unveiled, while I was unafraid,
and at long last the child within could heal.

If I could find the Grail, all things would be
as they were meant to be, as I had dreamt,
when just a boy playing in lustrous trees,
those sacred summer days—before the serpent.

From a Classified Location in England

by Brian Yapko

Dear Jim—my son—I write from far away.
From England, Spring of 1944.
June first! That means you're six years old today!
So happy birthday, son! And many more!
Please know my heart is with you on this day—
You and your mother—as I fight this War.

I can't believe that two whole years have passed
Since I last saw you, Jim! The photos show
You're practically a man, you've grown so fast!
You've learned to ride a bike, to catch and throw—
And all without me there. So stay steadfast!
'Cause you're the kindest, bravest boy I know.

I've missed too many moments of your life:
The start of school, your laughter and your tears…
Please tell your Mom I also miss my wife!
I count the days till war in Europe clears.
But I must soldier on to stop the strife
Of tyranny's dark curse of endless fears!

I've caught a bruise or two. A minor cut,
But—don't tell Mom the salty words I write—
I'm ready to kick Hitler in the butt,
And force his Nazi pals to say "good night!"
That day comes close… Jim, I can't share just what
My orders are. But know I'll fight for right.

If I don't make it home to you and Mom
There's something that I need to say to you:
You're watched by angels, Jim! Be strong, be calm.
I'd want you to begin your life anew.
Make friends, read books, find joy in every psalm.
Think for yourself and you'll grow straight and true.

I'm proud of you, my son. I'll always be.
But I must go now. Sure, I'm scared—but glad
To fight the Darkness so you can live free.
Remember me sometimes; please don't be sad.
If death must come, I face it willingly.
Just know, Jim, that I'll always love you. Dad.

POET'S NOTE: The Allied invasion of occupied Normandy on D-Day, June 6, 1944, was the largest seaborne invasion in history. Allied casualties on the first day were at least 10,000, with 4,414 confirmed dead. The operation laid the foundation for the defeat of Nazi Germany.

Bach in Heidelberg

for Marjorie

by Lionel Willis

Bach's chorus didn't leave us much to say
After the Easter Monday concert in
The Holy Spirit Church. Taking our way
Over the Old Bridge seemed like we'd just been
Visiting Heaven. The flooded Neckar's din
Blurred the cantata fading in my head,
As memories of the recent passed grow thin.
Sensing my grief, at last our good friend said
"In us she still lives. Other gifts have wholly fled.

"Reams of Bach's scores are gone, yet reams remain
Of what may be the richest heritage
Ever bequeathed by one blessed human brain:
Incomparable gems on every page,
Now reverently passed from age to age,
But when the ink was fresh how roughly tossed
Aside as passé! And who now can gauge
How huge the treasure that was blindly lost
Of which our world must now forever mourn the cost!

"'What does it matter? Music comes and goes,'
Someone will shrug. Most music, it's true.
Like junk food for the brain, it fills up those
Who know no better. Like a sudsy brew,
Most music that the masses listen to
Dulls with emotion. How Mammon rejoices
To see earplugged consumers milling through
His bedlam of manipulated choices!
Most music's a drug. Why lament a few lost voices?

"But music isn't all the same. Bach's kind,
Where several voices join in harmony,
Demands one's close attention. All one's mind

Craves to sing too, following lovingly
How the selection moves from key to key
As one voice, then another, leads. A lot
Of mental discipline, as you can see,
Is both demanded by Bach's art and taught
By it. It celebrates the joy of taking thought.

"An enemy more fell than Time destroyed
Them as it has so much for which we care:
The randomness that hisses in the void,
Devouring hopes, laughing at our despair.
Wilhelm Friedemann, Bach's principal heir,
At first ably conserved his father's papers,
But his strength flagged. Depression, booze and bare
Necessity dogged him. Sold to the neighbors,
Fragments were torn for weigh bills and lighters for tapers.

"When we revisit a familiar song
We find new charms. In Bach we may well hear
New works, for every time we sing along
With well-known themes his further themes appear,
As if the very randomness we fear
Had somehow been enlisted by the soul
To make fresh anthems in the inner ear,
And through them all one lesson seems Bach's goal:
To show how every voice contributes to the whole.

"Polyphony had ruled four hundred years,
But now the Ariesque hung in the wings.
Wisely, Bach chose to polish what his peers
Despised as out-of-date: structure that sings
To brains that strive to think why dying stings."
Following Bach you promised me you'd wait
For me where good souls join the precious things
We've lost on Earth in that eternal state.
More cause to pray I too may pass through Heaven's Gate!

NECKAR: River in Germany

The Carnelian Ring: A Still-Life

Footfalls echo in the memory
Down the passage which we did not take
Towards the door we never opened
Into the rose-garden.
            —T.S. *Eliot,* Burnt Norton

by Joseph S. Salemi

I think of a walled garden, graced with trees:
Magnolia, fig, and cherry, while grapevines
(Just pruned enough to be under control)
Intertwine with trellises for shade;
And scent of lilac, honeysuckle hedges
Grown tall enough to grant us privacy,
With tended beds of roses in full bloom.

It must have a clear space for repose:
A table, marble-topped, on which there rest
Bottles of wine, a bowl of fresh-picked fruit,
Napkins, knives, cut-crystal antique glasses,
Should be surrounded by wrought-iron chairs
With cushions where my best and closest friends
Sit in the lazy shade of afternoon,
Comfortable, unrushed, totally at ease,
Drinking and speaking quietly of things
Known only to ourselves—our common past,
Dead companions, old catastrophes
That time with sutures, tourniquets, and salves
Has rendered now mere comic episodes.

Those are the circumstances, but add this:
We are all dressed immaculately. We wear
Our best clothes and accessories. And I
Have on my finger a carnelian ring
Set with heavy rose gold, and the stone's

Intaglio'd with a mystic, riddling sign,
Its occult meaning known only to me.

The garden is remote, and walled, and cool—
The trickle of a decorative fountain
Provides the backdrop for our conversation.
No crass, intruding stranger can come here
To violate this perfect magic circle
Or question what we know, or how we think.
My friends are precious to me; as each speaks
I listen attentively while my right hand
Turns the carnelian ring upon the other,
And think: *This garden is our mystic ring—*
Rose gold and carnelian with a mark
Undeciphered by my friends, and yet
Protecting them with talismanic force.

Fireworks

by Adam Sedia

The roar of battle rends the moonlit sky
With distant thunder as of cannons booming.
And bursting, crashing, popping salvos fly
Above the roar, the whirr of rockets zooming.

The din deceives, for when it yields to sight
A fire-dance fills the sky whose salvo jolts
Blithe, awestruck smiles to gasps of sheer delight
That brave the thunder to behold its bolts:

Starbursts of crimson, purple, orange, and green;
A blinding flash of white; a gold cascade
Or silver—sparkling fountains that careen
Like champagne spritz; bright clustered stars bright-rayed;

Or fire-sprites swirling in a spiral gyre,
Whistling as they whirl into nothingness;
Volcanic founts of sparks, pillars of fire
Ascending as they flare and incandesce.

The bursting fires so dazzlingly arrayed
By art into this eye-bewitching show
Rain in bombs and roar in the cannonade
That levels cities and lays legions low.

And in their thunder rings the din of war,
Echoes that inexorably portend
The clash of battle never looming far,
And bid the bursting sky-borne fires descend.

Hypnosis

a pantoum

by Judy Koren

Come over here, then, and sit in this chair,
Gaze at this candle-flame, empty your mind,
No need to worry, no need to beware—
I am so patient, so caring and kind.

Gaze at this candle-flame, empty your mind
Watch the flame flicker entrancing your soul,
I am so patient, so caring and kind:
You will obey me now, I'm in control.

Watch the flame flicker, entrancing your soul:
No need to worry, no need to beware.
You will obey me, now *I'm* in control—
Come over here then and sit in this chair.

Rejoice by Annie Stegg, 2010, acrylic on canvas, 16 x 13 in.
(www.anniestegg.com)

The Artist

by Shari Jo Lekane

Intuitive journey, subconscious creations
refuse to diffuse while the muse makes the choice
to infuse mystic magic with personal voice
giving birth to original manifestations.

Works will cement while fermenting with feeling
revealing a meaning unique to each eye.
"No one knows why," says the strange passer-by,
but upon contemplation the answer is healing.

Centripetal forces draw strength from within
showing structure and balance, a solid foundation,
knowledge and wisdom acquired over years.

Centrifugal force pulls from end to beginning,
talent and influence building formations
that seek inspiration and reach beyond fears.

Allentown Nights

by Sally Cook

Sometimes the nights were full of evil there.
Relentless searchers drove the block most nights,
While novices in bushes would prepare
As Lady Scarface told them of their rights—
Just how to rob with sharpened rattail combs,
And countless other petty cruelties—
Demanding money, breaking into homes.

And yet, each morning rose again; the breeze
Provided us with promise, and the light
Proceeded to protect. We walked with ease,
And wondered why so small a change, so bright,
Could cleanse the foul observances of trees
To fill the star-crossed corners of this blight,
Dismissing all the demons of the night.

House Sale

by Sally Cook

A wind of change flies through the halls,
Pushing the prints upon the walls
Askew, and tumbling each old quilt
And threadbare doilies, placed with guilt

In heaps upon the tables there.
A strange regressive waft of air
Speaks of the past, but not next year
When, doors locked, the raccoon and deer

Will wait for salt and peanut buttered
Snacks in vain; hear no words uttered.
For now each chattering china bird
Repeats the message it has heard—

Away with order, calm, and peace!
Some outgrown clothes, an old valise
Whirl in chaotic dance. Outside,
The glider rocks on its wild ride

With canopy at rakish tilt,
Evoking memories, like silt
Disturbed upon a river's bed
As ghostly as the walking dead.

Two cars' impatient engines hum
Beside a loaded rubbish drum
As handlers clear out every room,
Leaving a box much like a tomb.

Saint Joseph's Table

by Margaret Coats

The night before, old furniture
And scrap wood set afire
Smoke out the winter's wickedness—
An equinoctial pyre
Of habits, sins, misfortunes dark,
Succeeded by quick work
To level boards and flaunt a feast
Of charity superb.

A work of art, the table stands
(Its carpentry concealed);
The baker's craftsmanship looms large
In clever shapes revealed:
The cross, fat rings, bambino, braid,
A staff, a sheaf of wheat
Turned upside down is Joseph's beard;
His profile's glazed to eat.

Sesame tears adorn the bread
But sorrow comes with sweets
Of almond, anise, wine, and fig;
The Lenten banquet meats,
Salt anchovies and fresh sardines,
Deck pasta of renown;
Fennel and dandelion greens
Boast sawdust crumbs for crown.

The saint once long ago gave rain
When there was desperate need;
Now families, churches, clubs, and towns
Turn laborer to feed
Whomever comes—a naughty trick
To break the solemn fast,
But solemn joy just once this day
Is strict as penance past.

Knurled oranges add a finished touch;
The lilies' royal smell
Is doused with holy water drops
And vibrant voices swell,
Te Joseph celebrent caeli
In sturdy gratitude
To a virile father fostering
His yet uncounted brood.

TE JOSEPH CELEBRENT CAELI: Let the heavens celebrate you, Joseph (first line—shortened—of the best known Latin hymn to Saint Joseph)

Cascading Nation

by Jon Parsons

Now not so much a nation as a place
for pushing through a brute cacophony
of cultures in discordant synergy,
dismissing calm consensus, wit, and grace
as if considered discourse would abase
befuddled masses yearning to breed free
and manifest a new world destiny
while tumbling headlong in this teeming race

one cataract of countless souls who flow
an arcing aching ecstasy of flight
and moiling mists, as falling waters might
cascading take a form we think we know

so protean Niagara remains
unchanged by waters drawn from many rains.

Slow Verse

by Lionel Willis

No need to rush: These lines have lots of time.
They never face a hanging at first light.
They can take pains to whittle a neat rhyme
And years to get each subtle cadence right,
But they can never take the hero's part,
They can't shout in the streets what must be said,
Convey the words to mend a breaking heart,
Brandish the silent challenge of the dead,
For those demand another sort of pen,
One improvised to staunch a gush of blood,
A hasty scrawl that won't be scanned again,
A jagged shriek of warning in a flood:
The page that speaks for all the quickly crushed
Reads like a wind, but this one won't be rushed.

Mother and Child by Gustavo Ramos, 2020, oil on panel, 15 x 12 in. (www.gustavoramos.art)

I Am with Child

by Michael Charles Maibach

> For all my life
> I felt alone—
> Out on the road,
> As well as home.
>
> I saw couples
> With children near,
> Filled to the brim
> With sweetness dear.
>
> But then it came,
> This life in me.
> I am "with child"—
> Now all can see.
>
> It's in my walk,
> My softer voice,
> My warmer hand,
> My surer choice.
>
> I sleep so well,
> And rise with ease,
> No longer sad—
> My soul at peace.
>
> This comes from God,
> His best gift, sure.
> This life in me
> Will now endure.
>
> For all my life
> I felt alone.
> Then this dear child
> Came to my home.

Let It Bleed

by Johnny Payne

My family believes a puzzle piece
is missing, that it's me and if they snap
it in, the family will have peace.
The picture will be whole. They'll close a gap.

But as I stand outside, I see no space
to fit me in. The edges have gone smooth
where there were lines, effaced into a place
I visit, but its presence doesn't soothe

the sense of absence, or the phantom limb
they scratch when vanished live flesh tingles
while they touch, and say "This leg was him
whose sudden loss now stings our fingertips."

That puzzle is one that still puzzles me.
And looking on, I learn that I'm not free.

The View from Space

by Ellie Strano, high school poet

My helmet gone, I float among the stars
As weightless as my lungs deprived of air
Asphyxiating slowly, I am far
From all I love and anyone who cares.

The stars are dead already: cold and hot,
Like burning funeral torches in the sky
Their lifeless eyes of fury hurt me not,
I am forsaken, destined here to die.

The world ends not by fire or by ice
It does not end at all, but slowly spins
As I, among stars' fire, turn to ice
And pray that God absolves me of my sins.

My body swallowed in the black abyss
I close my eyes and welcome death's cold kiss.

Poppy

a pantoum

by A.S. Chuba, high school poet

A vase of poppies on the table there,
Twelve years have passed, all white is now her hair.
A shadow running up the path she sees,
Her son has come! Her end to miseries.

Twelve years have passed, all white is now her hair.
She missed him much, with fear she couldn't bear.
Her son has come, her end to miseries!
With grateful heart, she drops down on her knees.

She missed him much, with fear she couldn't bear.
A shadow running up the path she sees.
With grateful heart, she drops down on her knees.
A vase of poppies on the table there.

Pier

by Leland James

Set firm in waters indigo and gray,
she is a promontory; into mystery a way,
a mooring fast, a compass true, end stop
upon the rim of ever-changing day:

abiding sound, steadfast upon her rhythmic
stays, a seasoned way, prelusion span,
timeworn gateway into the main, a toran
into a sea sown deep with atavistic

shifting rhyme—there a maiden vessel sails,
makes fast her lines upon new tides, explores
the untried shore, high cliffs, seabirds, salt air,
the haunt of unseen lands, a world newborn.

Awakened from this childing air I hear
a carol from the shore, an echo of the pier.

An Intelligent Cup of Coffee

"That must have been some cup of coffee!" —Charles Ellik

by Daniel Kemper

The coffee spins and I am not the same.
The time in which I move is muddy, turns
around my breath, and steams. As sunlight
came here perfectly, some perfect still returns
and carries new reflections of my eyes
back to my eyes. *Oh nature and O soul
of man,* your flawed, but *linked analogies*
exceed my breath. But does this little bowl
of brown, suspended dust in its own deep
demitasse of Turkish grind comprise "me"?
My own reflection blinks away its sleep
and turns. Am I the same? No eye can see
how dust could move to personality—
and yet it moves—to immortality.
What moved the primal dust to me? How do
I say? And since mere dust like me has got
a soul, then I can ask not "What?" but "Who?"
And likewise ask, "Who made that dust? Has not
The Deep called out to deep? The coffee spins
and I am not the same. How far beyond
all utterance: The Name where it begins.
No ear can hear, no mind can comprehend
*(though not the smallest atom stirs or lives
but has its cunning duplicate in mind)*
the good God has in store, lavishly gives
and has lovingly, thoughtfully designed.
Wrapped in reflections spinning in clay jars,
the love that moves the sun and other stars.

Regrets and Repercussions

by Peter Hartley

Inconsequential are the things we do
Sometimes, or things we don't, we don't know why.
So will we wonder far too late and sigh
To think that if we knew we could undo
The past before it starts, begin anew.
How many of us would instead deny
The imminence of fate to justify
Inaction in the face of all we knew?

So often small mistakes may have such long
Far-reaching repercussions that amaze
In hindsight. If we knew where we went wrong
Before we did so, might we change our ways?
If only we were able to return
To where we were. But would we ever learn?

Reclamation Project

by C.B. Anderson

I never thought I'd live to see the day
When men and women feared to speak their mind,
Nor did I think that what they had to say
Would pique the general ire of humankind.

But I was wrong—it happens all the time,
And I have lately learned to keep my mouth
Shut. Nowadays, the most egregious crime
Is speaking truth; the world is going south

Into a netherland where nothing's what
It really is: what's false is true; what's true
Is false; discernment has no value. But,
If I may make a point, the sky is blue

When we wake up, and all the birds still sing
The Sun into its place up in the sky.
The clocks still work, and almost everything
Is just the way it was in days gone by.

This Earth, though not my friend, is yet my mentor;
Although we've disagreements now and then,
It's still no place I'd hesitate to enter,
Despite the irritating ways of Men.

Nest Egg

by C.B. Anderson

The things for which I hoped have come and gone:
The power to express a cogent thought;
Ability to wake at break of dawn;
Approval from a nearly perfect wife;
And will to execute what I've been taught.
But this is not to say that all is lost
Within the precinct of the twisted life
I've lived, for many turns are yet to come.
Eventually—I keep my fingers crossed—
I'll realize a windfall benefit
From old investments that I made. In sum,
I'm less dependent on my bank accounts
Than on tenacity and native wit,
Which I possess in copious amounts.

The Arrow of Time

by Brian Yapko

The arrow of Time flies relentlessly straight—
Exacting, unyielding, it never comes late.
It flees to the future appallingly fast
Disdaining the present, discarding the past.

It offers no mercy, it harbors no trust;
It causes whole cities to sink into dust,
Reduces tall mountains to undulant hills
And darkens fine art with the drear Age instills.

Time makes flowers brittle, it desiccates trees;
Time's arrow carves canyons and dries up the seas.
It turns sap to amber and wood into stone.
Divorced from all pity it turns flesh to bone.

The arrow of Time yields to nothing on Earth
Not the weeping of death nor the cries of new birth.
It robs me of peace with an edge which cuts deep
And rushes me forward to unwelcome sleep.

Hardship and Destiny

to the Class of 2021

by Benjamin Daniel Lukey

The time is now at hand; the bow is bent
To shoot you forth across the open sky.
And as you think on what these years have meant,
You may know where you wish to land, and why.
Or else you may believe you hold the bow;
An arrow cannot aim itself for flight.
You've chosen paths to take; I hope you know
Their ends are far beyond our power of sight.
Some days, the way before you will seem bleak;
Pursuit of happiness is arduous.
Persist—and you will find the joy you seek.
Please don't forget to send some back to us.
    We'll miss you so much more than we can tell,
    But we are proud to bid you all farewell.

Elemental, My Dear

*Slight air and purging fire, the first my thought,
the other my desire.*
   —Shakespeare, "Sonnet 45"

by Alison Jennings

I am of air and fire wrought, though I
am drawn to water like a dowsing rod.
Carousing through thought's realm, I am a fly,
zigzagging near and far to find a god
who'll both inspire and accept the need,
intermingling brashly with each other,
to stoke a fire that my heart can feed.
Newness blazes forth from one another,
while water fills the lakes within my soul
and soothes the charring edges of my mind.
What does not dampen ardor, keeps me whole
as fire battles air for equal time.
 These forces make me who I am, and yet—
 I fear sometimes that they are more a threat.

I Don't Know Why I Think Things Will Get Better

by Geoffrey Smagacz

I don't know why I think things will get better.
I'm always holding on to flimsy hope.
I've held it since I was a young go-getter
before the downward slope.

Is wishful thinking printed on our genes?
Before we crawl, has nature made it so?
To want things right by any and all means?
I don't presume to know.

Or did my mother give this curse to me?
No turn I did was ever good enough.
She'd say, and this is not hyperbole,
"You're made of better stuff."

Or was it God that stamped it on my soul
and left me unfulfilled and wanting more?
There is a place where I can never stroll,
on Eden's ancient floor.

A few more days in bed; it won't be long.
To shroud the hospice's incessant hum
I'll raise the volume on Sinatra's song,
"The Best Is Yet To Come."

Disambiguation

by Anna J. Arredondo

As in the dawn the nature of the beams
Of light invading chambers—how they glint,
Conceal with shade, or paint with rosy tint—
Reveals the day, not as it *is* but *seems*,
So, in the natal cradle of our dreams,
From the beloved's eye we aim to mint
A wealth of useful knowledge, sign and hint,
And draw our own conclusions from its gleams.
    Though in the morn the outlook of the day
      May soon beyond a doubt be ascertained
        By boldly drawing back the veiling curtain,
      Where feelings are concerned, some of us may
        So dread the risk of being dashed and pained
          We find it better *not* to know for certain.

Sonnet 1 (In Theory, Real)

by Hannah Yee, high school poet

Are dreams confined to stars or stars to dreams?
Both full of mysteries and seldom clear,
Restrained, yet free to dance in vivid streams
Of consciousness, of life and fire and fear,
For isn't that how all these are perceived?
Compelling to the science of our hearts,
But so far-fetched, too strange to be believed,
Too vast to comprehend and, yes, in part,
Quite frightening, unknown and unexplored.
Still we traverse the pathways of life's game,
Our stars, our dreams, just guides that go ignored,
For aren't they controlled and used the same:
    Rough seas of light, ideas to study, feel;
    Just kindling for our thoughts, in theory, real?

Peace and Love Are Here

by Sandi Christie

The world is full of suffering and pain;
We wait in fear for death to walk our way;
We look for anyone that we can blame
Projecting fear and hate along the way.

Where fear has entered, love can never be
And with it, peace of mind is gone as well,
For all we see now is insanity—
The mind that lives in fear must live in hell.

For just one moment, cast your fears away
And ask for peace and love to fill your mind.
Cast every judgement out without delay
And shine the light of love on all mankind.

The resurrection of the mind is near,
For fear has gone and peace and love are here.

Right on Cue

by David Whippman

Who took the years? Who stole the time away?
Where did it go? I just don't understand.
There were so many things that I had planned,
Such clever dialogue I had to say.
Have I been written out of my own play?
The years seemed plentiful as grains of sand—
Most of them, now, have trickled from my hand.
Am I a dog who never had his day?
I know that I was meant for better things,
Yet now the spotlights dim, the music stops.
No one applauds as I step on the stage.
I spent my whole life waiting in the wings—
To find a play with neither cast nor props
Nor any lines, only a blank white page.

Meditations on Ecclesiastes

by Cynthia Erlandson

Inquiry

"What profit has a man for all his labor…?" —*Ecclesiastes 1: 3*

None knows what all his work accomplishes;
What one begins, another finishes
A different way. Or, fools may come in after
He dies, waste life in lust and drunken laughter,
Abandoning the place he built. None will
Recall his arduous efforts or his skill.
This inescapable absurdity
Asserts the depth of earthly vanity.

Perplexity

"And this also is a severe evil, that just exactly as he came, so shall he go. And what profit has he who has labored for the wind?" —*Ecclesiastes 5: 16-17*

We cheer each birth—yet, as man comes, he'll go—
Naked, as he arrived. The womb is narrow
From whence he comes—as is the grave, where sorrow
Pervades the winds of vanity that blow
About the burial ground, where neither sparrow
Nor man can fall whose Maker doesn't know.
Of all the things he's worked for, none will follow
Him to another world. This world seems hollow
To those who mourn his loss; the here and now
Cries out, "Futility! This life is shallow!"
The place of grief surpasses that of mirth;
Therefore a death seems better than a birth.

Irony

"There is a vanity which occurs on earth, that there are just men to whom it happens according to the work of the wicked; again, there are wicked men to whom it happens according to the work of the righteous." —*Ecclesiastes 8: 14*

Whoever humbly works beneath the skies
With perseverance, thrift, and industry,
Should be rewarded. Why do some, then, rise
By evil? Even worse: the irony
Of those who fall by virtue, is a cause
For philosophical perplexity.
It seems to work against all prudent laws
To give to those who've done no good the prize
That should have been bestowed upon the wise
And diligent, however many days he
Labored for posterity. How crazy
To keep back payment from the just! Absurd
Among the things that we have seen and heard,
This system certainly appears insane,
And magnifies a world that seems in vain.

Limerick

by Joe Tessitore

I have lived my whole life about me
And at last I can finally see
   That my choice only smothers,
   Life is all about others
And the truth really does set you free.

Honest to God

a rondeau

by James A. Tweedie

I do not know why Sarah died;
I only know her parents cried
Such tears as only parents shed
When infant children die in bed—
A grief they did not try to hide.

At birth a tumor deep inside
Her brain was found and verified.
They asked the doctor, "Why?" She said,
   "I do not know."

She died in spite of all they tried
And I, as Pastor, could have lied
And made up "why" their child was dead
But chose to speak the truth, instead,
And in all honesty replied:
   "I do not know."

Apocalypse

by Joseph S. Salemi

The fractured sky splits, flaming at the edge—
The earth heaves upwards in explosive wrath.
No eye can bear the clay-caked risen dead
Sleepwalking through the streets in blackened shrouds.
The seas turn into boiling, viscous blood
And everywhere, unending trumpet-blasts,
Swarms of gnawing locusts whose foul wings
Buzz and whine like sand-filled, shaken rattles.
Disgust and violation choke all throats;
The stench of chaos, havoc, and disorder
Pollutes the nostrils of a baffled world.
This is *Apocalypse,* or *Revelation*—
A tearing-down, a showing-forth, a leap
From what we are to what we must become.

II. LOVE POEMS

The King and the Beggar-maid by Edmund Leighton, 1898, oil on canvas, 64.09 x 48.39 in. The tale tells of a king disinterested in marrying until he meets a beggar-maid on the street. He immediately falls in love with her, proposes, and brings her to his palace.

Anyone But You

by Anna J. Arredondo

The phone may ring;
The call will bring
   Anyone but you.

The mail will come;
It will be from
   Anyone but you.

A text may buzz;
I'm sure it was
   Anyone but you.

Oh, this is dire;
I don't desire
   Anyone but you.

My Sonnet as Texted

by Carl Kinsky

Her face, uplit as she scrolls through her phone,
no feelings shown, she wears light like a mask.
Have we two lives we share? Is each one's own?
Afraid that I know, I'm too scared to ask.
I stay in shadows, silent, statue still,
and watch her phone's glow wash across her face.
A dancing light, love alters course at will;
at whim, it changes distance, strength, and pace.
Her Facebook friends share their most liked new memes.
She stares intensely. She can't know I'm here,
can't know my fears, just theirs, their hopes, their dreams.
Remote though she appears, she stands so near.

My sonnet's sent. She smiles. Shade turns to shine.
I'm part of her life while she's all of mine.

December

by Peter Hartley

Two years ago it didn't seem as cold
As this. But then her heart was warm, and she
Would make this house a happy place to be.
Where once the rhododendron would unfold
The garden weeds exert their stranglehold.
The lawn is sodden wet, the rowan tree
Has shed its showy berries. Here we see
Its boughs are bare, so barren to behold.

The dying and the dead surround me here
Till in the spring the flowers reappear
In all their glory as they do each year
To bring us happiness and bring us cheer.
But still I mourn in this December chill
For she will not come back, nor ever will.

My Lips Have Kissed Her

by David D. Irby

My lips have kissed her lips. Now I know why
the timid sun arises with each day.
I understand what moves the birds to fly
and why the trees within the breezes sway.

My lips have kissed her lips. I can't deny
that it has moved me to my very soul.
The rules of intellect do not apply.
One kiss, and I have lost all self-control.

My lips have kissed her lips. I must comply
with wishes that my heart cannot ignore.
My feelings now can surely justify
that I go back and ask her lips for more.

A Rose and Me

by Mike Bryant

My words, like models, only pose
As simulacrums of this perfect rose.
   No one can know or comprehend
The rise and flow of love, the weft, the bend.
   For love is what we know and feel—
The deathly lows, the height of heaven's zeal.
   Intensity is what I see
In every moment that you look at me.

   So, please accept this long-stemmed rose
Which reaches out to you, the one I chose
   In softened sighs, and read the note
That answers all the questions that you wrote.
   I hear you *sotto voce* here
Within my mind and see your blue eyes clear.
   I'll always hold your memory—
The stem, the bloom, your fingertips and me.

Obsession

an Alfred Dorn sonnet

by Tamara Beryl Latham

As candles gently glow in amber light
The picture centered high upon the wall
appears to take a life form of its own.

Yet, thoughts of her are stronger on this night.
He views her fleeting image in the hall,
as he sits drunk, contented and alone.

He rises, sets the glass upon the sink.
She appears only when he takes a drink.

Yet thoughts of her are stronger on this night
He stumbles through the hall to hesitate
then tremble as his body chokes with fright

to see her form begin to levitate,
sprout angels' wings then suddenly take flight,
while he remains to curse the hand of fate.

Magnificent Outpouring by Laura Westlake, 2021, oil on board, 12 x 9.5 in. (laurawestlake.net)

Brighter Horizons

by David Watt

I have seen the sunrise over
An expanse of brightening sea
As I wandered like a rover,
Long before you came to me.

I have seen the sun rise early,
In its haste to pack a punch,
So the city's hurly-burly
Settled down in time for lunch.

I have seen the sun rise scarlet
With its garish face in smoke,
Like a stogie puffing harlot
On the lookout for a bloke.

I have seen the sunlight struggle
When midwinter morns hung bleak;
And the birds stayed in to snuggle
Up together, beak to beak.

I can't count those mornings, weary,
When the sun rose far too soon
For my eyes, still tired and bleary,
To regard her light till noon.

I have seen the sunrise stolen
By the depths of placid lakes,
And regretted brilliance swollen
Washing out to silver flakes.

But no matter place or season,
Every sunrise now is grand,
For the one important reason—
That your face is close at hand.

Sunset

by Michael Miller

A life alone is at its center bare,
A quiet conversation with myself,
A single, threadbare suit I always wear,
A volume set aside upon life's shelf.
A time or two fate's hands would find me paired,
Awakening to partnership each day.
A coupled time where thoughts and deeds were shared,
An interlude that kept dark thoughts at bay.
A pleasure past is left as dispossessed,
An absence added to my solitude.
As life is loaned by time then repossessed,
A canvas bright at birth becomes grey-hued.
   To once more find a love would ease my soul,
   To have a peer to hold would make life whole.

Though Worlds May Die and Silent Be

by Roy E. Peterson

Till rolling seas cease heaving high,
The starry nights stop passing by,
The universe is wrapped in flame,
And there is no one left to blame.
    Until then? … You're my loved one.

Till sun no longer makes a day,
And earth will never get a ray,
The quiet coldness of the earth
Bespeaks a lonely universe.
    Until then? … I'm still not done.

Though worlds may die and silent be,
We still have an eternity
To be together, on and on.
The words like death and dying gone.
    Until then? … We've just begun.

L O V E...

by Susan Jarvis Bryant

It's not a dozen scentless hothouse roses.
   It's not a chocolate-box of sweet cliché.
It's not the scorching kiss that lust imposes
   To lead the fired and fevered flesh astray.
It's not an aphrodisiacal dinner
   Or sighs in dizzy highs of fine Champagne.
It's not a pricy pledge placed on a finger
   If *always* means till youth and fervor wane.

It's words all selfless souls have thought and spoken.
   It's songs that soar above the spinning sphere.
It's heaven's gift, a glorious golden token
   That shines its rays when days are dark and drear.
It's ears that hear the fear beneath our laughter.
   It's eyes that warm us when our world is cold.
It's hands that hold us here and ever after—
   Beyond the age when bones and hope grow old.

It's never been a borrower or lender;
   Its bliss is given unconditionally.
Its flame burns with a beauty, truth and splendor
   That blazes in the bond that sets us free.
It's rest when we are weary, lost and lonely.
   It's peace when here on earth we're ash and dust.
It's forever—it's our cherished one and only—
   Love's our pleasure… Love's our savior… Love's our must.

You Are Too Far from Me

by Arthur L. Wood

Send me your love for I've nothing to write,
And my words are vacant or ugly—
I slept through the morning, I raved out the night,
   And you are too far from me.

I feel the entropy taking the world,
Send me your love while loving can be—
The past is finished, the future dissolved,
   And you are too far from me.

A wall looms round this plaything of gods,
From the center there's only so far we can flee,
My days are the same, small talk and nods,
   And you are too far from me.

Send me your love, my outlook is bleak,
I try to be patient with my poetry—
I know my predicament isn't unique,
   And you are too far from me.

The river we stumble, shuffle, or skate o'er,
Melt it must, then flow to the sea,
I'm quiet in England, your love I wait for,
   And you are too far from me.

Marriage as a Dance

by Reid McGrath

Everything that's living craves Existence:
Plants stretch for soil, sun and sky, and rain.
What creature will not devise a defense
against destruction and impending pain?
Of entities with constituent parts,
like ecosystems—engines which burn fuel—
my heart is one. But in my heart of hearts
you are ensconced like an illumined jewel.
More potent than petroleum or wine,
I crave your fuel that helps my engine run.
Beatrice led Dante nearer to the Son
as you help me back to my Maker's manse—
Who is Existence; He designed the dance
and called it "Good." His ducks were in a line.

III. HUMOR

Fire and Ice by Jacob A. Pfeiffer, 2019, oil on panel, 9 x 9 in. Visit the artist's website at jacobapfeiffer.com

It's Fall, Y'all!

by Susan Jarvis Bryant

Autumn is here and I'm swathed in a sweater,
   A snug fluffy scarf and warm mittens.
My Ugg-cuddled feet have never felt better;
   These boots are as cute as soft kittens.

Autumn is here and it's chocolate I'm sipping
   With melted marshmallows galore.
Pumpkin-spice candles are glowing and flickering,
   But PHEW… when I open my door…

Autumn is here and the temperature's soaring;
   Cicadas still screech in the trees.
Leaves are spring-green and the fierce sun is roaring;
   I wilt in the sweltering breeze.

Autumn is here and the heat greets and beats me.
   My woolens are hurled on the deck.
Never mind cocoa, toss ice in my sweet tea
   And rub some sunscreen on my neck!

Autumn is here yet I feel Summer simmer;
   She mocks me from sizzling skies—
The chance of an autumn in Texas is slimmer
   Than hairs on a butterfly's thighs.

The North Pole's on Lockdown

by Susan Jarvis Bryant

'Tis the night before Christmas; it pains me to say—
The North Pole's on lockdown before the big day.
The elves have been furloughed and fester in bed.
The toy factory's folded and Rudolph is dead…

Poor Prancer and Dasher and Dancer are lame.
An arrow struck Blitzen and Cupid's to Blame.
Dear Donner's a goner and Comet's unfit
And Vixen is on a rotisserie spit.

All starry-night flights pose a threat to the globe—
St. Nick and his sleigh failed a federal probe.
"He'll sully the chimneys, leave germs on lit trees!"
Says grinchy old Grouchy, the Chief of Disease.

'Tis the night before Christmas and who gives a damn—
The season is missing the bearded main man!
Since Santa's accused of the worst type of vice,
He's not fit to judge who is naughty or nice.

Be warned, the "new normal" is gift-less and grim;
Kris Kringle's gone bust and he's hitting the gin.
He's blurry and slurry with no *HO HO HO*
In ermine-trimmed crimson with nowhere to go.

The saddest of all is his scant welfare check—
So meager it won't buy a present or deck
His bleak, barren hall with one bough of green holly,
Resuscitate Rudolph or bring back our jolly!

A Tale from the City

by Joe Tessitore

They've worn my patience very thin
So I wear my mask upon my chin
"Nose exposed!" a stranger's cry!
"Brains in chains!" my swift reply!

I sneezed and hit her with a snot.
She fainted right there on the spot.

Vitamin DC: In Praise of Dark Chocolate

by Jeff Kemper

When I crave from my enclave something to eat
(Not apples or peas or muffins or meat)
I steady my stare at my pantry's archive
And spot a great lot that'll keep me alive.

In my haste for a taste of the finest cuisine
I select my elected morsel between
Other sorts of sweets, numbering four or yet five;
For indeed, I need some DC to survive!

So I fly at my diet with quiet repose,
Tearing open the wrapping, sweet meats to expose,
Popping into my mouth a delightful brown hue
To masticate morsels and morsels to chew.

The exemplary frill of this thrill forbids haste;
I desist from my chewing to savor the taste
Of dark chocolate rocking and rolling my mood
And blocking, consoling—all cares to occlude!

My imbibing transcribes the good savor to health.
When DC descends to my gut's commonwealth;
To the depths of my being, digested, refined.
It is good for my heart and my total mankind.

I will sing and will ring adulations galore
To the nurture that casts me on heavenly shore,
For the chocolate block of that food I decree
Is the dark one I christen "Vitamin DC."

Obit: English Pronouns

by Jan Darling

Dear friends we gather here to say goodbye
To words once used to speak both truth and lie.
The *he* and *she* and *his* and *hers* and *mine*
By *zie* interred forever at *zir* shrine.
No more can we know *zim* or *ver* by gender
Just judging by the personal pudenda
It's *zis* or *hirs* or *vers* or *eirs* or *ters*
Don't be surprised—incertitude occurs.

When the Alphabet of Egos started out
The pronouns that we used were put to rout
Good useful words were sent the way of "gay"
A word once used for happiness and play.
Then, sex assigned at birth did, inter alia,
Define us more or less by genitalia.
But now we hear there is a kind of speaking
Describing diverse kinds of gender leaking.

I love the bastard kids of dear old English
The "how to use" that oft afflicts in Chinglish.
No language has a more expansive heart
Than the language handed on from dear Old Dart.*
It gives me all the pronouns that I need
To address myself to any faith or creed
I don't need words that show a sexual preference
When he and she provide my basic reference.

Chromosomal complication's not so rare;
Just a differentiation in your share.
Does this require a new approach to grammar?
Or do they simply think it adds some glamour?
Pronouns tell us who's who and what is what
Ignoring what you *do* with what you've *got*.

Who owns what and which and why is made clear
From there do what you like with your own gear.

If we let our English pronouns be coerced
Our total mother tongue will then be cursed
Our English Grammar murdered by these fools
By gendered language spread through government schools.

Say no to *hirs* and *zim* and *ters* and *vers*
Consign them to a multi-gendered hearse
Declare yourself in favor of plain speaking
Untrammeled by the speech of gender leaking.

---

*OLD DART: Refers to England: the river Dart in Devonshire enters the sea at Dartmouth, site the Royal Naval College. Officers returning to England after a tour of duty referred to returning to "Old Dart."

A.B. Brown as Lord Byron, photo by C. Driskel, 2022.

Cup in Hand

an arch anacreontic rejoinder to Blake

by Talbot Hook

The world in a grain of sand
Is nothing to a cup in hand;
And heaven in a wild flower
Is nothing to a lover's bower.
Infinity within one's palm
Cannot compete with liquor's psalm;
Eternity you bid me hold—
Sound advice, for when I'm old.

The Effect of Lawsuits on TV Commercials

by Russel Winick

The long commercial all but says
"This medicine can kill.
But nonetheless we'd really like
For you to use our pill."

Parents' Drop-off Kisses

by Russel Winick

Our house is near a bus stop, so
Today I watched who came.
The moms and dads and children
Either talked or played a game.

To black and white and Asian kids
Each parent's kiss brought shame.
We hear so much of contrasts now,
But mostly we're the same.

Plight of the Formal Poet

by Russel Winick

With her sterling work rejected
She was feeling rather sad,
But the formless tripe selected
Turned her mood to almost glad.

Sonnetized

by K. Irene Rieger

"Why poetry?" My chair leans in his chair
And slides me a sabbatical-swelled smirk.
The past nine months I'd shouldered all his share
So he could spend his patriarchal perk
In penning pap not destined to see light.
"A couplet is a manageable cup
"To nurse while nursing newborns in the night."
"Not good enough!" The old man shuts me up.
"For poetry's a calling—a vocation!
"And rhyming's so old fashioned—risible!
"Such arbitrary rules curtail creation!"
The sonnets' strictures may not be permissible,
But to them I entrust my rage, nonplussed,
The bulldog bitch contained, but only just.

Lahaina Mynahs

by James A. Tweedie

The droppings of a thousand Mynah birds
(While nesting in a Maui banyan tree)
Descended on my pre-teen daughter. Words
Cannot describe her abject misery.

Her shoulders, arms and hands were plastered white
As were her t-shirt and her auburn hair.
In shock, she stood there screaming—what a sight!—
With gobs of dripping bird crap everywhere.

No doubt you've heard the phrase, "Shit happens!" Well,
In this case it most literally did.
Humiliated by the birds from Hell,
My daughter was a miserable kid.
Today, she laughs, though memories remain
When tropic skies dropped poop instead of rain.

Bring Your Own

by James A. Tweedie

The invitation put me in a bind;
I couldn't figure out "BYO**B**."
And though I searched for one I couldn't find
A good excuse to not RSVP.

The "BYO" I knew meant "Bring Your Own."
But what the final "**B**" meant wasn't clear.
Within its cryptic acronymic zone
It could mean "**B**ourbon," "**B**ottle," "**B**ooze," or "**B**eer."

I didn't think it meant to bring my "**B**aby."
Or my old "**B**oyfriend" ought to come along.
Could it have meant a "**B**ullwhip" or, just maybe,
A "**B**ratwurst," "**B**agel," "**B**aklava," or "**B**ong?"

But in the end, instead of being boring,
I brought a "**B**ugle" I kept under wraps.
Then pulled it out when people started snoring
And closed the party out by playing taps.

A Slight Deviation from the Canterbury Tales

after Chaucer's Prologue and other poems

by Brian Yapko

When that April with his showers sweet
Made mud fields out of every field and street
And caked with blackest moss each flower pot
As made our hero grumble "Out, damn spot!"
So did the West Wind make our hero leery
That date night might become a midnight dreary.
Wont to argue, would his date dispute
Of man's first disobedience?—And the fruit
He bought to woo and win her went to rot
(Cheap-purchased off some lady from Shalott.)
Our hero met his date. Alas! Dismay!
For she was more rough wind than buds of May!
Although she walked in beauty like the night
She had a scolding tongue—a waspish fright!
Lilacs in the yard withheld their bloom
When she complained—the very voice of doom!
They walked till evening spread against the sky
But strayed. She mocked him with a glittering eye.
Foul-mouthed in the frith, her anger grew.
Whose woods these were he truly thought he knew
But he was wrong. Well, better to be lost
Than loved, he thought. This date packed too much cost!
They argued underneath a poison tree.
Two roads diverged. The best was not to be.
There was no help and so they kissed and parted.
Free! Our hero was not broken-hearted.
The vales rejoiced! No albatross in sight,
He ambled gentle into that good night.

NOTE: This poem won the First-Liners Poetry Contest that required a poem to begin with a famous line of literature. Judged by Cynthia Erlandson.

COVID and Travel

from Shakespeare's play Richard III, *Act I, Scene I*

by Julian D. Woodruff

Now is the winter of our discontent
Stretched out through spring, to summer, likely fall.
In masks and social distancing we've spent
Over a year, and now we're facing, all,
Arm twisting at its finest to get tested
And vaccinated not just once, or twice,
But more. Refuse, and we may be arrested,
Or fined, or both; all that may not suffice.
For instance, travel has for months been hard.
You want to board a plane or cross a border,
It's "Oh, but you don't have a vaccine card."
Patience and options, too, are growing shorter.
The train?—nix! Next, they'll take your car by force.
Then might you beg, "My freedom for a horse!"

NOTE: This poem won Second Place in the First-Liners Poetry Contest that required a poem to begin with a famous line of literature. Judged by Cynthia Erlandson.

Split Nursery Rhymes

Jack Be Nimble … Jack Be Quick

by Joseph S. Salemi

Jack be nimble
With that fuse—
A long one is the type to use.
If it's long, it does the trick.
If it's short, well …
Jack be quick.

Hickory Dick … ory Doc

by Susan Jarvis Bryant

Hickory Dick
Let's make it quick—
All done in the tick
Of a tock!

You won't cure the sick
With a needle that thick!
Is this shot compuls-
ory Doc?

NOTE: These poems were selected by Joe Tessitore who created the Split Nursery Rhyme challenge, which requires beginning and ending with a line from a nursery rhyme.

Starbucks Villanelle

by Matt Hsu, high school poet

Will someone call an order for Elaine?
I have a bunch of stuff I need to do.
The wait today is driving me insane.

This one dude wants a pinch of sugar cane.
I can't believe he's holding up the queue
Will someone call an order for Elaine?

I'm standing here and all I feel is pain.
My legs and feet are slowly turning blue.
The wait today is driving me insane.

Barista, please, I'll gift you some champagne.
You don't want me to leave a bad review.
Will someone call an order for Elaine?

I ain't the type of person to complain,
But it's not like I asked you for a choux.
The wait today is driving me insane.

I want to drive a fork into my brain.
It cannot take this long to make cold brew.
Will someone call an order for Elaine?
The wait today is driving me insane.

The Rhymes-with-Orange Challenge

I Found a Magic Ring

by Luca D'Anselmi

I found a magic ring that makes up words.
It's multicolored: red and green and orange.
I picked it up and mustered all my corange
and slipped it on. How strange. I had a birds-

eye view of all our English words. Two-thirds
were uninvented still, and I was soarange
over streams of etymologies still pourange
into seas of future meanings, wild herds

of colorful profanities like whorange,
strange cities where New Englishish is spoken,
and universities where wokes speak Woken
and dye their hair in glorange and in blorange,
which scientists illegally will clorange
in labs someday from red, green, and orange.

In Cockney

by Brian Yapko

In cockney if 'arry says "apples and pears"
'E's really describing a walk down the stairs.
If I 'aggle a bit with me "trouble and strife"
I'm really addressing my dear 'appy wife"
So now will you join me for gin and an orange?
Oh, blimey, I've broken the lock and the door 'inge!

Orange

by Sarah Hills

The problem, it seems, is that there's hardly a word
That isn't plain wrong or extremely absurd
That rhymes with that fruit, with its name and its hue
It's easy to rhyme with red, pink, green and blue
But what about orange, yes, orange I ask
For me this has been an impossible task
Porridge and Borage and lozenge aren't right
And for weeks now I've tried with all of my might
But nothing is coming that isn't absurd
I really just think that there isn't a word.

NOTE: The above poems were selected by the creator of the Rhymes with Orange Challenge Cheryl Corey.

On the Australian Desert Town: Station View

by David Watt

Where meager rains are tinted red
From dust the Western winds have borne,
The publican to stranger said:
"We're fortunate that here is shorn
A class of wool unique in hue—
The pre-dyed fleece of Station View.

"And as for boundary fence and post
That creeping sand is wont to reach;
Their disappearance lets us boast
Possession of an inland beach—
Devoid of water (that is true),
But few can swim in Station View.

"The spinifex is not a pest
As most outsiders seem to think,
Because its tumbling from the West
Draws lonesome cowboys in to drink;
And that's what keeps our town afloat—
The whisky sales these weeds promote.

"And though our buildings look rundown
To those who favor formal brick,
We cultivate a trend in town
That tends towards a shabby chic;
Where peeling paint is a la mode,
And faint the praise for bland abodes.

"The frill neck races in the spring—
Now that's a sport of boundless thrills!
To see them run around the ring
On skinny legs, displaying frills,
Brings tears of joy and Cheshire grins;
Especially if your lizard wins!

"Astronomy, you'll be amazed,
Is all the rage on cloudless nights;
When homemade telescopes are raised
By locals spying Martian lights—
Seen redder here than cherry pie
Thanks to our gritty, ferrous sky.

"What's that? I'm just a mental case!
This town's an unremitting dump!
For you, we'll very gladly place
An extra hairy nettle clump
Inside your city-fitted britches.
Then, as you flee, beset by itches,
We'll say: 'One less to share our riches!'"

FRILL NECK: the Frill Neck Lizard, or Frilled Lizard, is a species in the family Agameida. These striking creatures are endemic to northern Australia and New Guinea.

SPINIFEX: a genus of perennial coastal plants in the grass family.
This is one of the most common plants growing in sand dunes along the coast of Australia.

B-Boy by Mario Loprete, 2017, oil on concrete, 39 x 31 in.
(instagram.com/marioloprete)

A Can of Worms
by Susan Jarvis Bryant

I saw it in the writing on the wall.
I couldn't help but read between the lines.
I knew that pride would come before a fall;
A bold and blatant sign of troubled times.
Caught within the crosshairs and red-handed,
(I'd Champagne tastes and lean, beer-budget means)
I champed upon the bit as I was branded
A mad dog torn apart at fraying seams.

The milk was spilt, the shit had hit the fan.
I bit the dust then came back from the dead.
To leap straight in the saddle was the plan.
I didn't cry, I forged ahead instead.
I travelled as the crow is apt to fly;
As pleased as punch, as happy as a lark.
Crazy like a fox and just as sly,
I brought home hocks of bacon in the dark.

I burned my bridges in the midnight oil.
I blew my trumpet till my face turned blue.
I busted chops and guts and reaped the spoils;
Turned over gleaming leaves all spring-green new.
I learned that all is fair in love and wars,
The finest medicine—guffaws of laughter,
A golden goose and nest egg in my drawers
Would make me oh so happy ever after.

These days you'll find me resting on my laurels,
Grinning like a cat who's lapped at cream.
No axe to grind; I'm done with heyday quarrels—
Until the cows come home I'll live the dream.
To those who say my life is naught but cliché,
I say I've stepped outside the box to think.
One has to break some eggs to make a soufflé—
If an ass drags me to water, I won't drink.

A Spider in My Room

by Radhika Bianchi

In the corner, there's a spider
Between the ceiling and the wall.
Its legs are long, its body small,
Seeing it there my eyes grow wider,

Fearing it to be the kind
Of spider I've been warned about.
I swallow back a piercing shout
And try to see the telltale line

On its back that makes it look
Like a tiny violin.
But the line, so very thin,
Evades my eyes in that dark nook.

I do not dare approach too near,
Anxious it might jump on me,
So stripy legs I cannot see,
Nor the six eyes that I fear.

Is the deadly Brown Recluse
Or its gentle predator—
The Tiger Spider—by my door?
I just can't tell. Oh, it's no use!

But just as I decide, it seems,
To kill the spider anyway,
With a fatal blast of spray,
I remember several dreams

Wherein I, like a fighter,
Lost in labyrinthine halls,
On bloodied knees and elbows crawled,
Followed by a giant spider.

Now, as I turn my gaze behind,
I'm tormented by the doubt:
Is it there to help me out?
It doesn't move and I'm inclined

To think that maybe I mistook
The chilling semblance of its skin
For its character within.
But then it speaks and I am shook

By these eerie words I hear:
"Tranquil you will never be
Because you came from inside me,
And I exist in you, my dear.

But you are, sadly, too obtuse;
The truth you run from and ignore—
That you and I, down to the core,
Are both the Tiger and Recluse—

Means you abhor your darker themes;
Just look at how you crawl away,
Trying to keep my touch at bay,
So, I come to you in dreams."

Before the monster gets away
I squeeze the can and spray, and spray!
And though the spider falls, reduced,
I fill my room with toxic juice.

I stumble out and slam the door,
Coughing, hands and knees to floor,
To the bathroom, wash my tears,
And when I glance up at the mirror

In horror, I jump back to see
Six beady eyes staring at me!
I blink and take another look,
Confirmed: my face her likeness took,

And limbs increased from four to eight.
Forlorn, I mourn my beastly fate.
Now I see without a doubt
The truth in what she spoke about.

When, again, in dreams I spy her
In her nest, I crawl beside her.
Cradling me ever tighter,
She whispers, "Incy, Wincy Spider."

In Memoriam, W.S.

by Jack Murel

Most righteous, good, and well-intentioned peers,
I write these lines to bury Shakespeare—not
To praise him—and here prove the reason dear,
Unhallowed scriptures now are cast as naught.
To read or not to read his treasured plays?
On "Not" you now insist, and by your leave,
I'll list his crimes, the Bard's most heinous ways:
That Jews and Christian kings feel want, taste grief,
When pricked do bleed, how so-called shrews untamed
Live free, of brave, new worlds where mercy is
Not strained, of plays in plays, what's in a name,
On true love's course, and deaths bought with a kiss.
For all these mighty wrongs and more, be gone!
Fie, poor Bill! We've known you well too long.

Poetry by Paul Erlandson, 2022, oil on canvas, 24 x 20 in.
(www.paulerlandsonart.com)

Tales of Tales of Tales

by Luca D'Anselmi

We can't remember. After years of war
that thing once known as "poetry" was lost.
We know there was a Greek named Robert Frost;
we don't know what "pentameters" were for.

In rotting libraries the lame and blind
burn offerings to Hecuba and Seth.
They brew a postapocalyptic meth.
Perhaps it's poem-like; it blows your mind.

They sing about the ancient poetry:
how once a woman listened to the tales
whispered by a snake with silver scales,
and plucked a golden apple from a tree.
What could it mean? We laugh and then feel sad.
If only we had poems like we had.

The Seven Dwarves of Old Age

by Roy E. Peterson

The seven dwarves of old age
   Have come to live with me,
But what could be the use of them
   Is more than I can see.

First Napper came and gave a wink
   And slept upon my bed.
Warm afternoons are quiet time
   When Napper is well fed.

The second one to slouch around
   Was Wrinkly, who's an elf.
I found him in a mirror when
   I looked upon myself.

Then Squinty, stumbling, came in next.
   His eyes could hardly see
The sell-by dates once printed on
   The food in my pantry.

One Rocky wanted exercise,
   So rocked upon my chair.
I bought two rockers for my den,
   So we can rock in there.

One Saggy sadly saw me when
   I had to take a shower.
He said that I was drooping flesh
   And had no muscle power.

One Freaky almost scared me when
   I tried to do some work.
I soon concluded Freaky was
   An angry foul-mouthed jerk.

And last of all, one Creaky crept
   And spoke from every bone.
With groan and moan and crackle-snap,
   He walked around my home.

So, what am I to do with them,
   Since they came here to stay?
Just move a little slower, give
   Them comfort every day.

Anglo-Saxon Limericks

by Peter Hartley

Alfred the Great

Alfred the Great was a shy king
Who found it not much to his liking
   Making do with cornflakes
   'Cos he'd burned all the cakes
While hiding his face from the Viking.

Sweyn Forkbeard

It is said that Sweyn Forkbeard
Would frequently walk weird.
   His lumbering limp
   Made him look like the wimp
The lusty old Bishop of York feared.

On the Cost of Doing Evil

by Lee Goldberg

I care not if the sky burns red and human flesh is seared.
I pray that all souls will just rot as many long have feared.

I wait for when the birds don't fly and locusts take the grain.
I hope the fertile soil dies from blood and acid rain.

I dream to see the lakes all boil and swollen throats stay dry.
I rejoice when the hopes and dreams of good men fade and die.

I laugh when fearful citizens are slaughtered like poor sheep!
I smile when orphaned children walk alone as they all weep.

My smile widens as the world becomes an ugly place!
I thrill while watching the destruction of the human race!

For I am one that loves the dark, and thrives on others' pain.
Misery and lack of hope are my most cherished gain.

I am a prince of evil, I revel in agony!
It's squeals of fear and suffering that set my spirit free!

I share all this on Facebook with some pictures to be seen.
I never get a single like; people are so mean!

The High Cost of Low Prices

by Mark F. Stone

Poetry is what I treasure.
Books of poems give me pleasure,
but my grief's been hard to measure,
   since I did some shopping.

"50 Famous Poems"—nifty!
Now on sale for just $2.50.
I should revel, since I'm thrifty,
   but my mood is dropping.

When great works cost just a nickel,
paying patrons will be fickle.
My career is in a pickle.
   Bargains—I resent them.

I had hoped to be excelling,
penning rhymes that are compelling.
Now I fear they won't be selling.
   Maybe I can rent them.

There'll be many poets frowning
when their verbing and their nouning
must compete with those of Browning.
   They will learn their rhymes' worth.

Dreaming large is sweet as honey.
Now my outlook's bleak, not sunny.
Write two poems for the money.
   You might have a dime's worth.

Looks like I'll be compromising.
Go ahead, be patronizing.
I will work in advertising:
   spams and Twitter spamlets.

There is just one consolation.
Poets can seek validation
through a laureate nomination
   in their humble hamlets.

Darwin's Cafe

by Anna J. Arredondo

As you dine on some fine macaroni,
Watch Eohippus turn into a pony!
   The primordial soup
   Is unsavory goop,
But it comes with a side of baloney!

Know How to Mow

by C.B. Anderson

You want to raise your rates, you say?
Your crying poor is killing me,
for what it's worth. Just yesterday,
when you were blithely billing me
for services you rendered on
a Saturday two weeks ago
—the mowing of my splendid lawn—
you seemed quite prosperous. I know
you have expenses you can barely bring
yourself to think about, such as the millions
you spend each year to keep your best Brazilians
from leaving your employ, but there's a thing
or two …. I hesitate to ride your ass,
considering the pressure that you're under,
but as a valued customer I wonder,
next week when you arrive to cut my grass,
if you might tell your crew to spare the hoses
left on the lawn, and mow *around* the roses.

Default, to a Fault

by C.B. Anderson

There are as many deeds I ought to do
As there are jobs in urgent need of doing.
My task is knowing whether to pursue
Them, or, too overwhelmed, to stop pursuing.

As numerous as shores that hem the sea
Are duties I am constantly annoyed
By; best of all the chores confronting me
Are those I may responsibly avoid.

Exercises in Frustration

by C.B. Anderson

Reticence

I knew at once she was the one for me
But wasn't sure I was the one for her,
And so instead of pressing on I waited.
If not for my perverse timidity,
Which ultimately led her to prefer
A forward loudmouthed oaf, we might have mated.

Pansification

Pansification: making something more like a pansy. Synonym: wussification.

Too soon the lilac bloom has come and gone,
Short-lived successor to the daffodil
And early herald of the garden phlox.
It's sad how much we have depended on
The shrinking violets lacking heart and will,
Whose school has no good answer for hard knocks.

Disengagement

My enemies have managed to get back
At me by simply leaving me alone
When I was poised to carry on the fight.
I would have faced the bastards at the crack
Of dawn, but when I rang their telephone
It played a message: *Have a lovely night!*

Twelve Chaucerian Limericks

for Paul Freeman

by Joseph S. Salemi

Some pilgrims went riding to Kent,
And here's how the journey was spent:
   As they traipsed through the dale
   They each told a tale
Of sacred or worldly intent.

Some of the stories were clean,
And others absurd or obscene.
   Whether gentle or lout,
   Each pilgrim cranked out
Tales noble or pious or mean.

One hundred and twenty all told
Was the number of tales to unfold.
   But Chaucer dropped dead
   Like a sinker of lead
And twenty or so's what we hold.

The Knight's Tale, chivalric and pure,
Was about courtly love, and I'm sure
   Folks listened politely
   But in truth (and quite rightly)
Found it dreary and hard to endure.

The Miller respected no rule—
He was vulgar, obtuse, and uncool.
   He showed no restraint
   In his tale of young queynte
And a fart in the face of a fool.

The Clerk spoke of patient Griselda:
How nothing her spouse asked repelled her.
   It was all just a test

And she proved herself best,
But I think any more would have felled her.

The Nun's Priest described a proud chicken
Whose dream caused his terrors to thicken.
    A fox came and grabbed him
    But the smart bird out-blabbed him
And so he's alive and still kickin'.

The Summoner solved an impasse:
How to equally share a fart's gas.
    For a friar had one
    He was given in fun
When groping around some guy's ass.

The Reeve's Tale is sordid and lewd
And shouldn't be read by a prude.
    While a bully was sleeping
    Two students went creeping
And his wife and his daughter were screwed.

The Wife of Bath married quite often
(Five spouses went off in a coffin).
    Her tale touched on strife
    Between husband and wife
And why female strength shouldn't soften.

The Pardoner told of three men
Who went out to murder, but then
    Their vile greed for pelf
    Brought them to Death itself,
And now they're in Lucifer's pen.

As for the rest, I keep still—
Their complexities baffle my skill.
    But read 'em, I'm urgin'
    (Whether harlot or virgin)
To get a medievalist thrill.

Prerequisites for a Trendy Poetry Reading

by Joseph S. Salemi

Casual clothes, streetwise but debonair:
Knit sweater, denims (slightly dishabille);
A tentative, apologetic air,
As if you told what you would most conceal;

Credentials of the avant garde, implied
In the unstudied flexion of your spine;
A contrapposto at the lectern's side
To match the supine slackness of your line;

Serious subjects, or some apt remark
That shows you *au courant* with modern times;
Personal torment, but conjoined with stark
Social awareness of our bourgeois crimes;

Above all else, an audience of sods
That hears its platitudes confirmed, and nods.

Dedicated to Those Who Give Up Chocolate for Lent

by Tonia Kalouria

A Box of Chocolates is like Life:
(That Mrs. Gump she got it right.)
You never know just what you'll get,
so take a chance: Jump in; don't fret!
Life's Bittersweet—both dark and light—
but with some luck, most bites you'll like.
It helps to read the Contents Card,
as some rejects lie smiling, scarred.
But *"C'est la vie"*: *"C'est si bon—bon,"*
and even though you get some wrong . . .
Still, *Carpe diem*!—and a plate.
Nosh choco-early, choco-late.

I Took a Notion (A Man's View)

by Norma Pain

I took a notion once in life,
To find myself a willing wife.
A wife who'd cook and clean and mend
And to my every need attend.
I had a momentary lapse
Within my mind that she perhaps,
Might meek and mildly do the chores,
Of washing windows, drapes and floors.
Of cooking breakfast, lunch and tea
And proudly serving up to me,
Delicious fare… no hint of diet,
And while I ate she would be quiet.
Never nagging or complaining,
Or require of me explaining,
What I do or why, or when
I might be home or not, and then,
Not be upset by mere digression,
Tolerant of my indiscretion.
Always loyal, sweet and yearning,
Trusting I'd be soon returning.
Waiting by the telephone,
So full of love for me alone.
She'd leave my slippers by the bed
And fluff the pillows for my head,
And if I was in need again,
She'd dutifully not complain,
But lay herself divinely prone,
Indulging my testosterone.
And after I was duly spent,
I'd hear no words of hurt resent-
ment, as I promptly fell asleep.
Nary a word, nary a peep.
She'd look upon me with devotion…
Once in life I took a notion.

But… life is hard to understand.
Things went not quite the way I planned.
The comely woman that I chose,
Was quite inclined to thumb her nose
At all my needs and raw desires,
Not caring much to quench the fires
That plagued my loins on many a night,
But rather she preferred to fight,
To grumble, argue and complain.
She'd look upon me with disdain,
Then serve me up her special roast
Of burnt, leftover beans on toast.
And should I dare to meekly utter,
My desire for toast…with butter,
Likely I would find instead,
The food arranged upon my head,
At which point she would turn about
And slam the door on her way out,
While I, adorned in beans and crust
Would watch the long-neglected dust,
Float upwards on the draughty force,
To settle in the sticky sauce.
Bewildered, I would do my part
And pray she'd have a change of heart,
But when late home and feeling chipper,
Nowhere would I find my slipper,
Or its partner, whereupon
She'd take two pillows… leave me none.
Then with a huff and puff and sigh,
While I not sure exactly why,
She'd turn her back in firm rebuff,
Implying that she'd had enough.
We split soon after we were wed,
I hired domestic help instead.

Jacob Cornelisz van Oostsanen Painting a Portrait of His Wife by Dirck Jacobsz, 1550, oil on panel, 24.39 x 19.39 in.

I Took a Notion (A Woman's View)

by Norma Pain

I took a notion in my mind,
That somewhere on this earth I'd find,
Just as in books and magazines,
A man of most substantial means.
He'd cross my path one fated day,
And never ever go astray.
He'd be good-looking, tall and slim,
From workouts at the local gym.
With clefted chin and dark brown curls,
And though the eyes of other girls
Would follow him admiringly,
His eyes would rest on only me.
I pictured him in perfect health,
With more than just a little wealth,
To buy me most expensive things,
Like Gucci bags and diamond rings.
He'd be mature and very wise
And never argue or tell lies,
But treat me with the utmost care,
Perhaps he'd be a millionaire,
And take me to the best hotels,
Where anyone who matters dwells,
To fraternize and shoot the breeze
With many fine celebrities.
I'd wear a Gucci gown that clings
With Gucci bag and diamond rings.
And underneath the pale moonrise
His love for me he'd poetize.
His touch would leave me feeling weak,
How cute the dimple in his cheek.
And never would there come a time,
When he would do white-collar crime,
Or send me out to work and toil,
For he would have huge shares in oil,
Enough indeed to buy me things,

Like Gucci bags and diamond rings.
And I'd be sure on countless nights,
To bring him sensual delights,
To make of him the happiest man
In all the world, would be my plan.
He'd look upon me with devotion…
In my mind I took a notion.

But… all those storybook romances,
Filled with charm and loving glances.
All those things that I had read
Were wrong, and what transpired instead,
Was unlike anything I'd dreamed,
Unlike the magic that I'd schemed.
And so, instead of wedded bliss,
My dreamy plans all went amiss.
Instead of all that money brings,
Like Gucci bags and diamond rings,
My washout wedded life began
And ended with the kind of man,
Who sat around in undershorts,
Unshaved, un-showered, watching sports.
For days on end he'd lounge about
And never take the garbage out,
Or vacuum, or pick up his mess,
Or feed the dog and cat unless
I lost control and screamed and bitched,
And threatened that we'd get unhitched.
And even then the lazy slob
Would not go out and get a job.
He'd smile a smarmy little smirk,
Expecting me to go to work,
To pay the bills, it wasn't fair
That he refused to do his share,
Or lend a hand, I don't know why,
Was he confused or was it I?
And little matter that I wept,
His promises were never kept.
He swore as sure as grass is green,
He'd always treat me like a queen.

He said his eyes would never wander,
Now I see him looking yonder,
Eyeing up the pretty girls
With Gucci bags and cultured pearls.
He promised me a solitaire
And top designer clothes to wear,
But all I got the last I checked,
Was disregard and disrespect.
No trace of all that money brings,
Like Gucci bags and diamond rings.

The Puppeteer
by Norma Pain

Oh hail the master puppeteer,
Controller of the strings.
The altruistic engineer,
Sagaciousness he brings.
With breathtaking dexterity,
He moves us all about.
From rich and famed celebrity,
To every down-and-out.

When he feels the time is right
He drives our limbs to action.
Manipulating day and night
Gives him much satisfaction.
And having no mind of our own,
We let him have his way.
As twice a year by strings alone,
He shifts the time of day.

Forward-back, year after year
Is clearly idiotic.
Yet why we do is still unclear,
We all appear robotic.
Our puppeteer is way off-track,
He makes life complicated.
Our inner clocks all out of whack,
All discombobulated.

Oh why this foolish pantomime?
What purpose this decree?
What use this faulty paradigm?
What help to you and me?
Our puppeteer has lost his charms,
We're dangling just by threads.
Our little wooden legs and arms,
Our little wooden heads!

Your Memory Starts to Slip

by Jeff Eardley

Now when you get to sixty-five, your memory starts to slip,
But when you get to seventy, you have to get a grip.
It's best if you can write things down to put your mind at ease,
To stop you losing mobile phones, remote controls and keys.

He headed for the village hall which lay just down the street.
Then walked into the crowded room and settled in his seat.
He sat next to a lady fair, her charms, they did beguile.
She said her name was Valery; she had a lovely smile.

It's then he started shaking as he broke into a sweat.
The lady sitting to his right was visibly upset.
He spoke to her with trembling voice, "I'm oh so sorry dear.
I don't know why I came today; I don't know why I'm here."

She said, "I feel the same as you: this ticket here I've got,
I know that it's for something, but I can't remember what.
I need to take a walk outside and have another think."
So they gathered their possessions and went out to get a drink.

They headed for the nearest bar, a cozy one at that,
And settled in a corner seat, so they could have a chat.
He said, "Now what's your poison?" She said, "Wine, and make it red."
But as he placed the order, he'd forgotten what she'd said.

He brought her back a jug of beer, which caused her to concur,
This fellow has a memory, a darned sight worse than hers.
Then as they left this busy bar, beneath the twinkling stars,
They couldn't quite remember where the hell they'd left their cars.

And so, at last they headed home, the hour was getting late,
And pledged that they would meet again to fix themselves a date
To go out for a special meal and share the Champagne cup.
They said they'd meet next evening, but neither one turned up.

Sonnets in Iambic Monometer

Selected by Paul Freeman

The Ghost

by Brian Yapko

> What sprite
> All night
> Must haunt
> And taunt
> This room?
> Of doom
> He groans
> And moans.
> I toss
> Quite cross
> Then shake
> Awake
> To see
> It's me.

Sonnets

by Angel L. Villanueva

> Give birth
> To words
> Of worth
> In thirds,
> And end
> your verse
> well penned
> And terse;
> But not
> With prose
> That's fraught
> With throes.
> Use rhyme
> Sublime.

Swoon

by Susan Jarvis Bryant

> The moon
> Unfurls.
> A bloom
> Of pearls
> Ignites
> The sky,
> Excites
> My eye,
> With beams
> So bold
> In dreams
> Untold…
> Of you…
> In blue.

Alas, Alack, Aloof
by Dusty Grein

> 'Twas at
> year's end
> I sat
> to pen
> iambs
> sublime,
> enjambed
> and rhymed!
> I tried
> a verse,
> but cried
> and cursed
> (methinks
> it stinks).

Thought Sport

by Jan Darling

> Your dreams
> Are lost
> In schemes
> Embossed
> With tears
> You shed
> And fears
> You dread.
> Your heart
> Beats still
> Then starts
> To chill.
> All sound
> Is drowned.
>
> But hear!
> The sound
> Of cheer
> Is found.
> Your thought
> was lost
> not chilled
> with frost.
> Free now
> To sing
> You vow
> To wring
> From storm
> Reform.

Pareidolia

Pareidolia: The science of seeing faces in everyday objects.
Apophenia: The human tendency to seek patterns in random information.

by Beverly Stock

Long-nosed creature
In my tile,
As I shower
All the while,

Nose that's bulging,
Smile half-cocked,
Jawline sagging,
Lips that mock.

Apophenia
I perceive.
Random objects
Stare at me.

Smokey lines,
Curves that trick—
I see faces
Real and quick.

Liquid soap makes
Lines refine,
But shower over,
They decline.

Gone again,
So we adjourn
Until my bathtime's
Next sojourn.

IV. CHINA

Imprisoned Falun Dafa Practitioner by Yuan Li, 2009,
oil on canvas, 41 x 30 in.

Connected

by Sasha Palmer

I'm Russian-born, live in the USA,
I'm Catholic, and Falun Gong to me—
A chain of cryptic hieroglyphs that say
Nothing of consequence; and yet I see—
Beyond the mystery—a familiar sight
As crouching tigers, hidden dragons fade
And all that's left is people, whom I might
Have known forever, closely; should I trade
Places with them, would I remain steadfast
In my own faith? Would I refuse to bow
Before the human idols? Would I cast
My fear aside? I do not know. Somehow
   I know this: when another victim falls,
    Don't ask for whom the bell of freedom tolls.

All Aboard

by Cheryl Corey

Two by two, the Uyghur stand in long
Lines. They carry nothing to call their own,
The final destination, a great unknown,
A distant, re-education labor camp,
To spend their days and nights in toil
For state and corporate masters. Kept as slaves
Until—that's if, escaping early graves,
They stoically renounce their faith as wrong;
Only then might they receive a stamp
Approving their return to native soil.

Winter Olympic mascots at Beitucheng Intersection: Panda returns to the "Panda Roundabout", photo credit: user N509FZ. (commons.wikimedia.org)

Sinister Symbols

by James A. Tweedie

O, how I wish I could write about pandas,
Cute, bamboo-shoot-eating, black and white pandas.
Furry and cuddly like overgrown teddy bears,
Roly and poly in singles or mating pairs.

Pawns in the game of First World foreign policy,
Used to help leverage trade and diplomacy.
Putting a happy face on China's image, while
Hiding a genocide under a panda's smile.

Pandas are peaceful and sweet beyond question;
Masking Red China's external aggression,
Blatant internal domestic oppression—
Pandas provide an effective digression.

Pictures of pandas displayed with a flair.
Even in Beijing's Tiananmen Square,
Hong Kong has pandas on loan to its zoo,
Visit the Spratlys, no doubt they're there, too.

Sadly, if pandas were Uyghurs, Tibetans,
Falun Gong, Muslims, or practicing Christians;
Rather than hailed as a mark of distinction,
Pandas would find themselves marked for extinction.

Pandas when seen as a PRC scheme
Turn out to be not as cute as they seem.
Sinister symbols of China's delusion;
Used to project a slick PR illusion.

The Heroes of Beijing

On the Movie Premiere of *Unsilenced*, Days Before the Beijing Winter Olympics

by Evan Mantyk

As great as it may be to send those hockey
Pucks on icy wisps of air into
A net as sweet as tightly guarded honey,
It is, at root, a childish thing to do
Compared to sending just one truth-filled flyer
Through fatal chills of government oppression
Into a hand and situation dire.
Ice skaters' spins and jumps do not impress
Next to the strength it takes to risk it all
For faith, tradition, what you know is right,
While on a globe as huge as you are small
Ignored by TV crews' high-powered light.
    On Mount Olympus whispers say something
    And laugh: "Who are the heroes of Beijing?"

A Day When Silence Spoke

This poem is commemorating the peaceful appeal of 10,000 Falun Gong practitioners for freedom of belief, in Beijing, on April 25, 1999. The appeal ended when practitioners left after being given empty promises of fair treatment.

by Daniel Magdalen

A "coup"? The will for truth. A "mob"? Respectful souls
Responsibility unites in heartfelt choice.
Their silence drowns the city's storm of noise. No voice
Shouts slogans. Silent, listen to infer their goals…

Their upright postures are by dignity sustained;
Petitions aim to right the twisted way of lies
That further twists the people's way of thought, and ties
Mass ignorance to fear, for hate through fear is gained.

If only for the hour, red agitprop machines
Give in to words of reason… As the gathered leave,
The atmosphere and place made clean beyond belief
Prove further what, in fact, true civic virtue means.

Still, ideology recaptures party minds,
Which go down roads redemption never finds.

Tank Man—Remembering The Unknown Rebel

During the Tiananmen Square Massacre, Tank Man (his name has been reported as Wang Weilin, a 19-year-old student) was arrested for "political hooliganism." Varying reports suggested he was either imprisoned or executed.

by Susan Jarvis Bryant

In Nineteen Eighty-Nine
He crossed the battle line.
The world saw courage shine—
   He took a stand.

His actions were unplanned.
Tyranny, be damned!
With shopping bags in hand—
   He took a stand.

He raised an open palm
With poise and grace and calm.
Without a trace of qualm—
   He took a stand.

With grit, he stood his ground;
Roared *Freedom!* with no sound;
Turned heads and hearts around—
   He took a stand.

He had his silent say.
They carried him away.
Although *he* knew he'd pay—
   He took a stand.

With everything to lose,
We're walking in his shoes.
Which one of us will choose
   To take a stand?

Family

for Xiaoyao Yin and her UK family

by Damian Robin

1

Loud thumps were more than company;
    front door as thin as any.
Mum walked across the noise to see
    each thump enlarge to many.

Then clumps of feet clacked on our floors
    with yaps demanding logins
To access private data stores
    they'd claw into like dog bins.

Though Truth's held high within my head,
    deep set, assimilated,
I hid my books inside my bed
    away from those who hated.
That night my naïve heart fell dead.
    My trust was confiscated.

2

My mother is exceptional;
    her parents had scant schooling,
Yet she was near the pinnacle
    of academic ruling

Before the persecution fell,
    before the mad negation
of Falun Dafa's moral swell
    that moved the Chinese nation.

Illustration by Xiaoyao Yin

They rubber-stamped her "criminal,"
   Restrained her body tightly,
They boiled her meals to minimal,
   her sleep to hardly nightly,
But could not break the golden shell
   of righteousness lit brightly.

3

My dad was also Falun Gong.
   Then came the persecution.
Confusion followed deep and long.
   No help. No restitution.

Relentless hàrassing grew tough
   from TV, papers, neighbors.
Worn down by terror's feats more rough
   than Hercules's labors.

Without Forbearance, shrank and died
   in Evil unforgiving;
he bent, he broke, he stepped aside,
   he's somewhere else and living.
The space between us far and wide—
   a torture rack unwitting.

4

My stepdad's lost. All's awkward, new
   as though he's lost his purpose.
In China, there was lots he'd do.
   Out here he's odd, a surplus.

He beat the state technology,
   cut right through blocks, diced danger,

Was locked up by the CCP,
   but here he's just a stranger.

His English conversation's crude
   so he earns basic wages
in Chinese kitchens, there preps food,
   repairs his life in stages,
Continuing what he's pursued:
   the Truth passed down through ages.

5

I'm now a Scottish refugee.
   I prize my parents' safety.
My ease with English kept us free
   and in a college lately.

Our family daily meditates;
   we heed an ancient calling.
Our spirit's one that cultivates,
   that rises after falling.

Because we all are refugees,
   For home we're always longing
But also build identities
   And soon find new belonging.
Amid life's harsh realities
   the Good alike are thronging.

The Game of Life (CCP Edition)

by Bethany Mootsey

We appreciate your purchase of this version of the game
That caused Mr. Milton Bradley to become a household name.
Though we cannot laud the methods for his capital success,
We endorse Life, with some updates, which we here below address:
First, the game begins in grade school, not in college as before,
After which you spin the spinner for your Gaokao score.
If you spin a one through three, the game is over, sad to say;
You must drive straight to the Poor Farm while your peers proceed to play.
For the kids still in the running, may your bribing hands be deft:
Your career will be decided by the player to the Left.
The next step, of course, is marriage, over which you'll have some choice.
Call your parents from the next room, and if they approve, rejoice,
Then begin to fill your car with little pegs of pink and blue,
But remember that the limit must be strictly capped at two.
As in previous editions, picking up Life Tiles is wise.
Now rewards will be more instant! See your Social Credit rise.
You can also penalize an infraction or mistake.
Use the camera in this box to patrol for goodness' sake.
As you drive around the board, obey the rules of every space,
Being sure to stay together. (After all, life's not a race.)
Count your money up and brace for this version's biggest twist:
Millionaire Estates is chosen through a predetermined list.
We sincerely hope these changes will create more joy than strife.
Happy driving, Party style, and enjoy The Game of Life!

GAOKAO: college entrance exam in China, which can be the sole determining factor in college admission and thus carries a high amount of pressure.

Dr. Wenyi Wang on the White House South Lawn, April 20, 2006

by Evan Mantyk

She shouts, "President Bush: Stop him from killing!"
Interrupting China's leader Hu,
Who looks around unsure just what to do.
All stand there stunned at someone who is willing
To speak when questions from the press are blocked,
When voices from the labor camps are choked
And all the world is in complicity soaked.
As if some naked man stood there, they're shocked
To see the Emperor who wears no clothes
And holds within his claws the butchered parts
Of people bound for sale at organ marts—
Then just like that she's stopped, and quiet grows…
The horror that has flashed before the eyes
Dissolves for now into a scene of lies.

The Devil's Definition

by Susan Jarvis Bryant

The Dragon's claw is slick with rawest red
From spoils that keep the greedy demons fed
With hearts from souls caught by the Dragon's eye
Sold to a world that buys the Dragon's lie—

A world that twists the gist of honest words
To hide the feasting beasts from senseless herds
Who bleat the mangled mantra of reform
Till genocide's "a different cultural norm."

When brains are washed in propaganda's guile
Then backs are turned on tyrannies so vile
The slaughter of the Falun Gong's dismissed
As devils deal in crimes that don't exist.

So never let the Dragon normalize
Barbaric acts all humans should despise—
Massacre occurs when ears won't hear
The sin concealed in spin that's insincere.

The Broken Kingdom

by Brian Yapko

Dare to look at China through a glass
Undarkly past the shining spires of steel
Which hide barbed wire. See the Party brass
Make laws coercing people not to feel.
See prisons sprout in sight of the Great Wall
And see the Yangtze clotted red with blood.
Regard the bones on which each garish mall
Is built—old virtues ground into the mud.
Then see our Friends of Freedom robbed of breath
Tormented to insanity or death.

Joyce described the sow that eats her young.
Well, Party leaders also eat their own;
They propagate the worst of Mao Tse Tung
Debasing freedom from a Marxist throne.
This harsh totalitarian regime
Which causes dissidents to disappear
Has squandered China's birthright with its scheme
To stamp out faith and hope with guns and fear.
Smash the temples! Plant informants! Spy!
Force men what to think. Then make them die.

Karma guarantees the Party's noose
Must one day strangle its own cold cabal.
Every act of torture, each abuse
Will bring it closer to its final fall.
Leaders that crush freedom into sand,
Who can't persuade and therefore must enslave
Must soon be driven from this broken land
Where they've failed to break the good and brave.
Inspired by the truth of wrong and right,
Falun Gong shall surely win this fight!

V. THE WEST

Morning Silence by Herman Smorenburg, 2017, oil on wood, 60 x 50 cm.
(www.hermansmorenburg.com)

This Present Madness

"To sleep! Perchance to dream; aye, there's the rub….."
　　　　　　　　　　　　　　—*Shakespeare,* Hamlet

by Cynthia Erlandson

I

The daily nightmare hovers: and each night
We pray to stay unconscious—not to dream
(Perchance to prophesy the planet's scream
At despots' brutal thefts and threats.) The plight
Of humans hangs half-hid behind a cloud
Heavy with thickening threats; betrays a theme
We strongly sense as some infernal scheme
Portending horror. Surely nothing good
Could lie in wait behind this stifling screen:
A sorcery we sense, though still unseen.

II

We wake into a bad dream every dawn;
The moments we can blessedly forget
This present madness that the world is in—
When we are free to have a pleasant thought—
Are fewer every day, and far between.
Increasingly, insanity reverses
Serenity; steals courage; cruelly curses
The watchful mind that's overwhelmed with what
Day's dreads reveal: advancing fearsome forces
Of chaos, thickening their plot. They strut
Proudly on the loud and hellish courses
That trace themselves on earth and in the brain.
Furious neurons race, transmitting pain
Of rage and grief, foretelling looming harm.
Darkening omens conquer calmness. Gloom
Closes quickly in and shrinks the room
While mental noise outshouts the clock's alarm
And, wide awake, we sense the coming doom.

The State of Art

by Sally Cook

The art world has completely turned around.
Now critics blind themselves, or close their eyes,
Shout how their contacts and their creds abound,
And laud sick rancid leavings to the skies.

Admiring excrement (which has been canned,
Shown, sold, and showered with the highest praise)
Investors gather, next to the best brand
Of booze, and clink their ice on crystal, gaze

At what they think is art. They linger here
(For trading nonsense objects is their game)
To worship stacked up bronze-cast cans of beer,
And urge the rest of us to do the same.

Once Rauschenberg's stuffed goat head in a tire
Took first prize at the Venice Biennale.
The best of all the ordure in the mire,
That goat stares out across a putrid alley

Of concrete cubes and ugly rusted beams,
Fake waterfalls, live trees choked up and wrapped
And all the other sophist, ugly themes.
Are there no artists left who aren't trapped

In lies and fakery and worthless schlock?
As pressure builds, there's bound to be a vast
Collapse of pretense, and a taking stock.
Art that comes from dung heaps will not last.

The Second Roman Empire

by Sally Cook

Those were the days, when Julius Caesar
Saw a country and would seize her,
And the busty Roman matrons
Ran the house and bossed the patrons.

Christians, at the least suggestion,
Gave the lions indigestion;
Later, Emperors used perversion
Like tennis, as a light diversion,

And citizens would sell their votes
And carried daggers in their totes,
And worshipped mostly anything;
Forgot to write, forgot to sing.

From Britain's shores unto Bohemia
Romans practiced their bulimia.
This sounds like what we've got today—
I think I hear a fiddle play.

Bonfire of the Vanities

"From Shakespeare…gushed a flame of…splendor…men shaded their eyes…"
—*Nathaniel Hawthorne,* Earth's Holocaust

by Bruce Dale Wise

Ah, yes, the human race had since become so brilliant that
they thought to banish all the fat, to burn the round Earth flat.
They thought to burnish inner cities; making no-go zones.
That way they'd rid the world of injustice, crimes, and loans.
They thought to banish the police so there would be no laws.
They thought to nix philosophers so there would be no cause.
They thought to cut out words from their vocabulary lists.
They thought to banish mathematics and the scientists.
They were so brilliant that they thought to censor common sense.
They outlawed man and woman due to their intelligence.
The happier they were, the more they burned, the more they lost.
They threw Nathaniel Hawthorne's words onto Earth's holocaust.

With Coffins at the Dover Air Force Base: 29 August 2021

by Bruce Dale Wise

On Sunday, Biden traveled to the Dover Air Force Base
to pay respect for thirteen service members who were slain.
But grieving parents of the dead were not consoled by him—
he kept on looking at his watch—and not so much at them.
One thought his empathy but hollow, disrespectful stares.
He chatted more about his own dead son than he did theirs.
They were owed more than they received; they still are owed a debt…
of gratitude, oh, those brave souls, we should not soon forget.
Go, stranger, tell your people these unfortunate ones tried:
obedient to shallow leaders, still they went, and died.

> David L. Espinoza, 20;
> Rylee J. McCollum, 20;
> Dylan R. Merola, 20;
> Kareem M. Nikoui, 20;
> Jared M. Schmitz, 22;
> Hunter Lopez, 22;
> Umberto A. Sanchez, 22;
> Max W. Soviak, 22;
> Nicole L. Gee, 23;
> Ryan C. Knauss, 23;
> Daegan W. Page, 23;
> Johanny Rosariopichardo, 25;
> Darin T. Hoover, 31.

The above soldiers were killed at Kabul Airport in Afghanistan in 2021.

The Afghan Plight

an alexandroid

by Satyananda Sarangi

The starlit sky is filled with smoke
        and men succumb
To dread, while folded hands invoke
        to overcome

This awful plight; yet prayers heard
        through fervid faith
Are breath for Satan. Death's preferred
        to blows that scathe

And wake the human soul. If eyes
        could only find
A route where dreams of peace can rise
        against the wind.

Habeas Corpus

by C.B. Anderson

Of those whose job it is to get results
It might be asked: to what infernal purpose?
Extortion, threats, felonious assaults,
And foul deceptions only scratch the surface

Of crimes they're always willing to commit
In order to accomplish what they're after.
Complaints of being roasted on a spit
Are met with unremitting rounds of laughter.

The means are justified by wicked ends
With no relation to the scales of justice,
And any vain attempt to seek amends
Is answered with a smug rejoinder: *Trust us,*

For we're not in the least like all the others.
Their extralegal powers shock and daunt,
So tell your sisters and your stubborn brothers:
If you are captured, give them what they want.

A lie that spares a life is justified
And certainly is not a mortal sin;
The bloody gurney on which freedom died
Is where a white untruth might save your skin.

Thriller

by Rita Moe

The world teeters daily on the brink
of disaster: mole-men burrow beneath
the White House, suicide bombers slink
toward the Hague, thousands squirm in the teeth
of giant mutant rats. The clock ticks.
Music swells. In the dark we savor the dire—
its salty taste, the mesmerizing flicks—
while humanity walks the high wire.
We know that in the eleventh hour will yet
appear the Man of Steel, the FBI,
the brilliant, gorgeous woman of science
to save the world. And then the true suspense:
the lights come up; we step, with blinded eyes,
into our own lives without a net.

Big Shots

by Mike Bryant

You're glad you've nabbed
The Covid jab
That's newly fabbed
In some large lab
Created by
The jaundiced eye,
The sneaky, sly,
Big corporate guy.
The slimy thug,
Our taxes sent
To make the bug
More virulent.
He's in with Xi,
Our enemy,
And Xi can see
Our liberty
Is in his way,
So he will pay
Those who obey,
Those who betray.
DNA
They fiddle with,
MRNA
Diddle with,
Your mind and life
They twiddle with,
Your country they
Have piddled with.
They're glad you've nabbed
The Covid jab.
…But why are you?

What Is Truth?

a pantoum

by Brian Yapko

To keep us blind and riven
You falsify the facts.
You will not be forgiven—
These are a tyrant's acts!

You falsify the facts
Promoting news that's fake.
These are a tyrant's acts—
Our liberty's at stake!

Promoting news that's fake,
You think you won't get caught.
Our liberty's at stake
As you assault free thought.

You think you won't get caught.
You make good people cower.
As you assault free thought
You flaunt abuse of power.

You make good people cower
To keep us blind and riven.
You flaunt abuse of power.
You will not be forgiven.

He Made That Choice

a rondeau

by Brian Yapko

He made that choice. He couldn't bear
The way he was, his face, his hair.
He felt he had to change his life,
To flee a selfhood that was rife
With shame he couldn't share.

Professionals who didn't care
Spoke words as empty as the air
On how to free him from this strife.
   He made that choice.

Now with mirrors everywhere
He sits and sobs. Some days he'll stare.
When he allowed the surgeon's knife
They said he'd make the perfect wife,
But now he's trapped in worse despair.
   She made that choice.

Lenin

by Duane Caylor

It's late. He walks the lonely corridor
in this part of the Kremlin with his cat
hammocked in his arm. He stops before
the door of every commissariat
that's still aglow and enters into each,
although he knows the commissars have gone.
Frugality is something he must teach:
he switches off the lights that they've left on.
He's like the cat he strokes so tenderly;
both have strong preferences, but weak affections.
His true love is an ideology
of which both wife and mistress are reflections.
At last, he finds the final burning light
and turns it off, inviting in the night.

The Lost

by Adam Wasem

The fog rolled heavy, down to blunt the day,
Sharp skyscraper tops dissolved into the gray.
Pale ghosts condensed, one here or there, lone, gaunt:
Scared eyes, blank masks, as if condemned to haunt
These empty streets that once were thronged with life.
They hurry with held breath still, afraid of the air,
The moist sweet air, which the tv claims is rife
With invisible disease. My son despaired:
"There's nothing left to live for!" To end his pain
He ran into the street, but no cars came.

Two weeks became two months, and then a year;
No family, friends, just endless broadcast fear.
The coiled spring snapped: The mob burst out in rage.
The boob tube babblers dutifully flipped the page,
And dubbed them "mostly peaceful" protests, straight-faced;
Behind them, beatings, deaths, whole cities ablaze.
As the flames and bodies piled higher, along with our grief,
The message was clear: No pardon, hope, or relief.

We're lost, bereft, like the fallen who slink in shame,
As not worth rapture when the Savior came.
We're seen, and run, but evil never tires,
And is baying for our heads. The cops retired,
Withdrawn by rulers safe in castles we built.
They saunter out, blissfully free from guilt,
To bless the mob for all they've set alight.
The mob descends; a fool few stand and fight.
The roar that rises, fading as we run,
Confirms our fears: Again, the worst have won.

We've reached the end, nowhere to hide, no escape.
The lucky will be beaten, maimed, or raped.
Not snow, but ash floats down to gently kiss
Us with the memory of the peace we miss.

A red—not sunset—grows; we turn, eyes grave,
Our only shield a prayer: *Let me be brave.*

Das Kranke Kind (transl. The Sick Child) by Fridolin Becker, before 1895, oil on canvas, 25.19 x 21.45 in.

Presently

by Lucia Haase

Today, I'm listening to quiet Time.
Today my porch enjoys an eerie calm
An echo in fresh air afar—the balm
Of bird song, happy nests—a kind of rhyme.
A moment's happiness within this clime
Seaside and lying 'neath a winded palm…
At least to me it seems a kind of psalm
That beckons thoughts as near as from the chime
Of my grandfather clock that's there inside
My house. It chimes a generation's sorrow
At what a border used to mean—a wide
Horizon line is not a thing to harrow
Or to bend in this quick life's long stride,
Which brings me from my porch to our tomorrow.

Don't Tread on Me

for Kyle Rittenhouse, acquitted on November 19, the feast day of St. Elizabeth of Hungary, patroness of the falsely accused.

by Joseph S. Salemi

Two enemies you faced down in a fight:
Canaille of leftist pigs for revolution
Who sought to kill you on that fatal night,
And then the malice of false prosecution.

Wild accusations from left-liberal slime
Who hoped to see you scourged and on a cross
Fueled outrage in those snots who called it crime
To fire back in self-defense. Their loss

Will now inflame the embers of pure hate.
They'll howl and screech in eardrum-bursting sound—
The poison in their guts is far too great
For any lancing other than a round.

But you did more than beat back those two foes.
You gave America some good fresh air—
You showed us how to pay back blows for blows
And not succumb to meekness and despair.

CANAILLE: pack of dogs, rabble

The Pox Fox

by Susan Jarvis Bryant

This silver-furred yogi of how to stay fit,
   This bespectacled guru of health,
Is a growly voiced sage of nefarious wit;
   A hoodwinking master of stealth.
This flip-flopping, truth-chopping, sly hypocrite;
This barefaced disgrace; demon prince of batshit,
   Is rolling in ill-gotten wealth.

This fork-tongued ace fudger of figures and facts
   Who wove the apocalypse thread,
Has backtracked on data and hacked with an axe
   Stale old omens for new ones instead.
This push-the-gloom doomster of grind-them-down sin
Is fleecing the country by selling his spin
   To the buyers of this brand of dread.

This weaselly wizard of mealy-mouthed care,
   This bender of useful-tool rules,
Defends years of breathing in mask-musty air
   In his mask-less charade to masked fools.
As the gagged sag on couches, evermore slouchy,
All maudlin and paunchy and evermore grouchy,
   The Pox Fox is gloating with ghouls.

On the Canceling of Dr. Seuss's *McElligot's Pool*

by Julian Woodruff

The book, we've been apprised, is most uncool—
Young Marco and the farmer by the pool,
Wits locked in friendly if serious duel,
And Marco sends the farmer off to school.

One Dr. Seuss, its author, we'll allow,
Here glorified in clever rhyme (and how!)
Imaginative fantasy; but now
The book will raise a most suspicious a brow.

To clarify, for any unaware,
This favorite of old depicts the pair
(The farmer and our Marco) both as fair—
White, in a word!—it's just too much to bear.

But Marco and the farmer aren't alone.
We see Mrs. Umbroso, too, is shown
Likewise Caucasian! In fact, Seuss is prone
To drawing people all so pale of tone.

There are exceptions, though—and here the man
As far strays from propriety as can
An illustrator. We must roundly pan
Much of his work. He's richly earned a ban.

The book in hand provides a good example.
The Innuit people he sees fit to trample
Through gross caricature. The proof is ample.
His squat Tibetan's but another sample.

It's sad that we must cancel Dr. Seuss,
But for his racist work there's no excuse—
So many instances of rank abuse.
Yes, there are traits to praise, but what's the use?

There Was a Free Nation That Swallowed a Lie

sung to the tune of "There Was an Old Lady Who Swallowed a Fly"

by Jack DesBois

There was a free nation that swallowed a lie.
I don't know why they swallowed that lie.
Perhaps they'll die.

There was a free nation hid under the bed.
That's what I said—hid under the bed!
They were under the bed to hide from the lie,
I don't know why they swallowed that lie.
Perhaps they'll die.

There was a free nation that stood far apart.
Wasn't that smart! They stood far apart!
They stood far apart to get out from the bed,
They were under the bed to hide from the lie,
I don't know why they swallowed that lie.
Perhaps they'll die.

There was a free nation that put on a mask.
Dare I ask? They put on a mask?
They put on the mask to stand closer together,
They stood far apart to get out from the bed,
They were under the bed to hide from the lie,
I don't know why they swallowed that lie.
Perhaps they'll die.

There was a free nation that took the jab.
How very drab—they took the jab.
They took the jab to get rid of the mask,
They put on the mask to stand closer together,
They stood far apart to get out from the bed,
They were under the bed to hide from the lie,
I don't know why they swallowed that lie.
Perhaps they'll die.

There was a free nation put back on the mask.
Again, I ask—they put on a mask?
They put on the mask despite the jab,
They took the jab to get rid of the mask,
They put on the mask to stand closer together,
They stood far apart to get out from the bed,
They were under the bed to hide from the lie,
I don't know why they swallowed that lie.
Perhaps they'll die.

There was a free nation that took the booster.
Crow like a rooster—they took the booster!
They took the booster and kept the mask,
They put on the mask despite the jab,
They took the jab to get rid of the mask,
They put on the mask to stand closer together,
They stood far apart to get out from the bed,
They were under the bed to hide from the lie,
I don't know why they swallowed that lie.
Perhaps they'll die.

There was a free nation that gave up their rights.
Without a fight—they gave up their rights.
They gave up their rights when they took the booster,
They took the booster and kept the mask,
They put on the mask despite the jab,
They took the jab to get rid of the mask,
They put on the mask to stand closer together,
They stood far apart to get out from the bed,
They were under the bed to hide from the lie,
I don't know why they swallowed that lie.
Perhaps they'll die.

There was a free nation that gave in to force.
They're dead, of course.

History's Tide

after the Epoch Times *series' How the Specter of Communism Is Ruling the World*

by Clara Huang, high school poet

History's tide brought us forth to this day,
A dark, sullen mist hanging low on display,
The Communist Specter's tail shriveled and feeble,
Yet tight is its desperate grip on our people.

A kingdom once reigning with luminous piety,
Now atheist wasteland, a fouled-up society,
The juxtaposition of ancient and new—
But watch as the tides of history renew.

Bask at the sedulous ornamentation,
The carefully handcrafted robes of the maidens,
In evident contrast with styles today:
The outrageous hairdos and denim decayed.

Once in the courtyards of school and academy,
Was scholarly ambition upheld with avidity.
Contemporary schooling, so farcical in comparison
Degenerate idealism's taint is embarrassin'.

Courtesy kept and character cultivated,
Innate human nature divinely-created,
A dignified bearing and language refined,
With chivalrous grace was a noble defined.

Yet in this new era where honor's displaced,
The crude and the vulgar are now commonplace.
Modern man's lost his original mannerism,
Can we still flee from the terrible cataclysm?

Traditional values are taking the stage,
Seize the deliverance before the end day.
Seek out Redemption the Creator now offers,
As virtues prevail and righteousness conquers.

Liberal Artists

by Sarban Bhattacharya

A little argument and then they hurt;
These liberals are so coy and sensitive.
They think they know all forms of decent art,
And claim consensus gives prerogative.

Their poetry requires subjective style
That craves an "I," a "me," a "my" or "mine."
Their views constrained to left side of the aisle
Require revolts of socialist design.

But oft their verse has splendid imagery,
Of camels flying high in azure sky,
Birds singing sweetly in a poetry…
As vapid as a tear a clown might cry.

For now, in colleges they reign supreme
All unaware here ends their Age's dream.

Racial Idiocy

by Russel Winick

My son was on a city team,
    Where two kids caught my eye:
Stefon—warm and articulate,
    And Marcus—risk deemed high.

I thought that I'd invite them to
    My law firm for a day,
And offer—if they seemed intrigued—
    Fine summer jobs, good pay.

But then another player's dad
    Who I thought was a friend,
Soon heard of my idea and
    Demanded that it end.

He called it a "white savior" stunt,
    And said that was "offensive."
Those shocking allegations made me
    Rather apprehensive.

I might have asked some white hoopsters
    To join in on the fun,
But on that team my son comprised
    The sole Caucasian one.

I'd had two white kids see my firm,
    For summers hired three more,
Though certainly I never thought
    To keep a racial score.

But in that space such accusation
    Flat intimidated.
And thus my planned out invitation
    To those kids abated.

Though I'm not sure I could have helped
    I'm sad this made me bail,
For Stefon's had just dead-end jobs,
    And Marcus is in jail.

Unintended Consequence

by Russel Winick

The African-American
High schooler had poor grades.
Folks worried for his future,
Seeing little effort made.

Some caring people spoke to him,
And urged it would be best,
If he worked hard to raise his grades
For college and success.

The youth replied that grades don't count
And shocked them with his spin,
That if he chose to go to college
Race would get him in.

Signs of the Times

by James A. Tweedie

"Post-modern" is the "ism" of the land;
Reality is hanging by a thread.
Objective truth? Rejected out of hand.
And God and moral absolutes are dead.

Ignore what ancient wisdom had to say;
What matters most is how a person feels.
And in the game of news the networks play
The dealer gets to choose which cards he deals.

Opinions, facts, and reason have no merit
Unless they are politically correct.
Deplorables are told to grin and bear it
When anarchists and riots intersect.

Both violence and mobs are tolerated
As long as they promote the "narrative."
But those who don't must be incarcerated—
For being woke is an imperative.

Our Constitutional democracy
Preserves, protects, defends each person's right.
But now our East Coast aristocracy
Sees everything in terms of Black and white.

Vast public lands that stretch from shore to shore
Are managed by what's called the "BLM."
Today those letters mean a whole lot more:
They claim our country's racist, not just "them."

To say our country's "great" is now taboo.
Support police and you might not get hired.
Your company now tells you what to do:
"Admit that you're a racist or be fired."

What happened to our land of liberty?
Where freedom once meant we could disagree?
Today, it seems, in order to breathe free,
We all must bow to Post-Modernity.

In liberty and justice, I believe.
But if they're lost to legislative theft
It won't be me who turns his back to leave,
My country is the one who will have left.

I Grieve Bleak Streets

by James A. Tweedie

I grieve bleak streets where handguns reign in terror
Daring inner-city residents
To duck and cover. Life used to be fairer
Years ago, when mayors and presidents,

Police, and everybody else refused
To tolerate a minor misdemeanor,
And those who broke the law were not excused
From prosecution. Neighborhoods were cleaner

Then, and safer. Children rode their bikes
At night, played stickball and most likely knew
The folks next door by name. Now no one likes
The way things are today—with men in blue

Defunded and considered out of fashion;
While perps and thugs are treated with compassion.

There Once Was a Very Big Lie

by Joe Tessitore

There once was a very big lie,
That our country refused to deny.
   While we did what they told us,
   To the Commies they sold us
And we kissed all our freedoms goodbye.

VI. NARRATIVES

Canto 2: Beatrice Visits Virgil in Limbo by Eric Armusik, 2017, oil on AlumaComp, 60 x 40 in. (www.ericarmusik.com)

Turbines

by Jeff Eardley

They lie in serried ranks above the strand.
These mighty, whirling monsters made of steel.
Where once, a couple wandered, hand in hand,
Not knowing what the future might reveal.
The murky sea rolls in from dawn till late,
You rarely hear the screeching seabird sound,
With drizzle tumbling from a sky of slate,
Upon the turbines spinning round and round.

These lovers came this way in sixty-three,
Without the wherewithal to own a car.
Before the Beatles very first L.P.
When no one ever traveled very far.
They gazed upon a hint of Paradise,
A cabin by the lonely sea they found.
But future Summers wouldn't be so nice,
When turbines would be spinning round and round.

Those sunny days, they came and went so fast;
Their footprints etched upon the drifting sand.
This couple weren't to know it wouldn't last,
Events would not unfold the way they'd planned.
For engineering work was taking place,
As night and day, the hammer drills would pound.
It didn't take them long, but now they faced,
Those mighty turbines spinning round and round.

She cried, "I have to leave, I cannot stay,
No longer will I find my pleasure here."
He gazed at her, then quickly turned away,
And poured himself another glass of beer.
With "Ruby" playing on the radio,
The morning that she took her love to town,

Her taxi-cab was waiting far below,
Beneath the turbines spinning round and round.

So now he spends his days in quiet repose.
The lighthouse throws its beam across the bay.
He thinks about the other life she chose.
She broke his heart the day she went astray.
He knows he must remain until the end,
When, come the day, they plant him in the ground.
He lights a cigarette and sheds a tear,
And gazes at the turbines spinning round.

An Incident on the Cornish Cliffs

by Peter Hartley

So many things were churning in his mind
When scrambling down the track towards the cove,
To take especial care or drop behind
Them both, decide perhaps it might behoove

Him to feign injury before his friends,
Avert the worst accurst day of his life,
Reverse his steps, the coward who intends
To yield before a hint of mental strife.

The voices in his head said "No, don't go,
For this is bluster, braggadocio,
And sheer bravado, putting on a show
For those below, as you must surely know.

The subjugation of your Everest
Does little to augment the sum of joy
On earth, no greater for your vain conquest
Nor growth in health nor wealth will we enjoy."

A self-indulgence this can only be,
Though steeped in needless fears and pointless dread,
The footpath led the way through rock debris,
The boulders all around them widely spread.

His friends, oblivious to fearful thought,
To nagging pains he felt deep down inside
His very core of being. Quite distraught
Was he beneath his overweening pride.

But credence he could scarcely ever give
To vague portentous hints, unwonted fears,
For dreams should not dictate the way we live
Nor night-time sorrows turn our days to tears.

And down the track three climbers made their way,
Between the granite boulders, heaps of stone,
And one of them would die that fateful day
Who climbed with two but sadly died alone.

He died alone that fateful day. He died
For no more reason than his self-esteem,
For nothing but that vain and arrant pride,
Could engineer fulfilment of his dream.

Too late by far for any to beseech
Them now. They raced, ignoring their sixth sense,
In haste to reach that great impending breach
That faced them and their misplaced confidence.

A bowline held the gear around each waist,
The crag grew near and one of them felt queer,
Too late by now to leave the wall disgraced.
No matter for these climbers who appear

Externally too very cavalier
To dread a fall. But one of them was full
Of fright that fateful day and fighting fear,
The hidden terror pounding in his skull.

He led the route straight up though with a lack
Of holds on fist-jams with the odd layback,
The tiniest of ledges let him pack
Two wedges in an overhanging crack.

And on pitch three he climbed above a nose
Of rock obtruding three yards into space,
With holds scarce big enough for twinkletoes
To grip the wrinkles of its granite face.

A micro-wedge gave little confidence
Jammed in the most exiguous of cracks,
Protection of such little consequence,
No spot to waver, nowhere to relax.

Towards a faint handhold he made a lunge,
The movement let his quaking foot slip free,
The wedge sprang out, he took a mighty plunge,
His arms outspread, his head towards the sea.

He made no shout to us nor flailed about
Nor scrabbled hopelessly, but seemed subdued,
For nothing could avail him now without
The kindly intercession of Saint Jude.

He made no shout, an utter waste of breath
For nobody could save him from this grim
Inevitable imminence of death,
Nor time had he to make his peace with Him.

No help for it, he plummeted earthbound,
A hundred feet he fell without a sound
To hit the rocks and debris on the ground,
The gulls abounding, laughing all around.

And still they laughed and wheeled about and still
Their raucous screams, unchecked by all they'd seen,
Crescendoed with a will, the air they'd fill
With shrieks and cries and everything between.

The gulls were gliding in their element
And floating on the thermals high above.
Their capabilities are heaven-sent
And shared by auk and petrel, hawk and dove,

But not by man nor any of his kind,
To avian propensities unknown,
For unpowered flight was never man designed
As Icarus and Daedalus had shown.

Three climbers on this Cornish cliff, one dead
And two forever chastened by his fall.
Forever both were filled with awful dread,
So cowed were they before that granite wall.

And surely better had he not been born,
The bliss of twenty years unmissed? Had he
Foreknowledge of that brutal end forlorn
Would he have begged to be or not to be?

His stricken partners on the crag no more
Could reach him than could soothe his dying groans
As he lay helpless on the shingle shore,
His shattered bones among the broken stones.

Internal Combustion—Vision for a New Dark Age

by Paul Erlandson

"Come with me, child, past all this camouflage."
"Is there a secret garden there, Grandpa?"
"Not quite. It's just a small, padlocked garage,
To keep out the enforcers of the law."

I keyed the lock, and lifted up the door
For just the time it took us to walk in.
The bulb inside was 60 Watts, not more.
I closed the door, and she began to grin.

"What's that, Grandpa? It's like Ezekiel's wheels!
Or like some dragon, full of majesty!"
"That, my girl, is called an automobile,
The way that God intended it to be."

"In old times, men were brave and women fierce.
We steered our own machines, commanded flame
With pulsing, violent roar I know would pierce
The souls of timid moderns, grown too tame."

"'Autonomous', back then, pertained to men
And women, whom these brute machines obeyed.
But now, we've yielded all control to them,
To these completely soulless cars we've made."

"May I please touch it Gramps?" she asked me, keen.
"Oh, I insist!" I said. "Learn every curve."
She moved with reverence to the machine,
And measured it with heart and hand and verve.

"Imagine now the thundering exhaust,
And rubber smoke from crisply chirping tires.

Imagine mankind not enslaved to Cost,
But free to race, the way the heart desires."

"These were not fashioned by some gamer geek,
But crafted out of elbow grease and passion.
Their power would make faint the modern meek,
And cause their sissy faces to turn ashen."

"These fire-belching dragons we adored
Commanded our respect but not our fear.
So, here's to Harley Earl and Henry Ford,
And everyone to ever grind a gear."

"Their spirit, child, I see it in your eyes,
Or else I'd not have brought you here to see
What others of your age would just despise.
But you will keep this car alive for me."

"Alive for some bright day when, once again,
The riotous act of driving is reclaimed.
Then, you will start this hot rod, and weak men
Shall gaze upon its glory and be shamed."

From Darkest Antiquity

by Martin Rizley

I. Ancient Ritual

A thousand brown feet burn on sand
In Pharaoh's funeral caravan.
By many a mirage they pass
Of phantom palms and pools of glass.

The princess moves as in a trance
While joining all the gods in dance,
For she on lotus fruit has fed
To walk among the kingly dead.

The shadow of Osiris falls
From lofty, silent, salmon walls.
Oh, what ancestral ghosts be hid
Within that awful pyramid?

The stones are lifted one by one,
And painted eyes blink in the sun,
Dark chambers yawn with mummies' breath,
Indifferent to another death.

The princess quits the rays of Ra,
Descends into the dismal craw,
As Nubian slaves go down in bands,
Led on by hieroglyphic hands.

A subterranean breeze blows cold
Within the torchlit tomb of gold
Where jeweled statues stand upright,
To greet the flickering firelight.

A priest intones a holy oath
That's written in the Scroll of Thoth;
He places then a scarab ring
Upon the casket of the king.

Wild shadows leap around the room
As all the living leave the tomb.
A golden cat sits idly by,
And watches with a diamond eye.

Now only one remains behind,
With listless, opiated mind.
The princess thus awaits her doom
Engulfed in everlasting gloom!

II. Cries in the Night

By night they come, on rough and rocky paths,
Without the light of stars or moon to guide
Their fearful feet upon this holy tide.
They come with gifts washed clean in cultic baths.

In swelling numbers, climbing winding ways,
The worshippers go up to that one place
Wherein there dwells a god whose dreadful face
Can drive men mad—who on his features gaze.

They come with precious offerings, therefore,
To please this fearsome deity, whose will
Can bless with riches, heal, torment, or kill
All who come near his altar to adore.

All through the night, in breathless awe they come,
From every part of Canaan, they ascend
On unillumined roads their way they wend
By abject terror stricken and struck dumb.

Atop the mount, they see the temple´s walls
As black as pitch, like some fierce beast of prey
Curled on its haunches, poised to pounce and slay
All those who desecrate its sacred halls.

Behold, the trembling couple drawing near!
They pass dark looming columns and behold

A sight inside which makes their blood run cold
And makes them wish they had not ventured here.

Beyond the open doors they can perceive
Through smoky haze a statue made of brass
With open belly through which things can pass
And arms outstretched its presents to receive.

From time to time, great flames of fire leap
Within the belly of the metal idol,
And from its arms, long chains—perhaps to bridle
A fitful gift—hang loosely in a heap.

Just then, a priest approaches from behind
And bids the pair draw nearer without fear
"Bring forth your gift, so prized, beloved and dear,
And know, to those who serve him, he is kind."

With trembling hands, the mother peels away
The swaddling clothes from her babe's tender flesh.
So lately bathed, he smells so clean and fresh–
How sweetly his eyes sparkle on this day!

The father takes him, hands him to the priest,
Who says, "I know it hurts to see him die,
But ours is not to question or ask why
When Moloch wants them for his sacred feast!"

With that, the priest draws near the glowing arms
To discharge swiftly Moloch's cruel will.
That night, loud cries go up on that dark hill
More chilling than a thousand shrill alarms.

III. The Plain of Dura

Beneath the noonday sun the young lads stand,
Like driftwood floating on an outstretched sea,
Or specks of light lost in a galaxy
Of countless stars; or like three grains of sand

Upon a beach. They calmly stand and wait
The moment that will soon decide their fate.

Surrounded by a multitude, they feel
Repugnance as their pious eyes behold
That horrid, ugly idol made of gold
Before which all around them soon will kneel
Upon a signal given by the king
To bow in awe before that wretched thing.

It rises up before them like a tower,
Its polished, shining form ablaze with light,
Its ghastly face designed to fill with fright
All who would dare defy its godlike power.
For gleaming fangs make clear the grisly end
Of those who would refuse their knee to bend.

That end is clear, for by the idol looms
A large brick furnace belching out black smoke
So thick and dense as to make armies choke
Upon its burning ash and searing fumes.
The scorching heat waves wafting from that fire
Burn with such force that some, too near, expire.

The fiery cinders swirling in the air
Remind the three young Hebrews of the pain
And terror that the king has vowed to rain
On those who would his royal creed foreswear
Or shun his idol forged by human hands,
Or firmly spurn his tyrannous demands.

The hour draws near when they must stand alone
As free men in a land of passive slaves,
Who by their words, would rather dig their graves
Than with a lying tongue, their God disown.
They will not join the crowds of cowering sheep
Who meekly bow to lies without a peep.

They look around, and feel both joy and grief,
Deep grief to see so many rendered blind

By hellish lies, which like strong fetters, bind
Men's hearts to fear and give them no relief.
(Held fast by fear, men sooner would comply
With wicked laws, than face the flames and die.)

Their joy springs from the knowledge that their God
Is always with them, so they can stand tall
Before proud kings and call on them to fall
In homage to the Lord, whom all must laud.
Such joy is theirs, despite the twinge of fear
They feel to have the heat of flames so near.

How blessed they are to know the Lord of lords!
To live in freedom from the nameless fears
That hold men hostage, without hope, for years,
Deprived of peace, which faith alone affords.
Thus, in their hearts, they vow, for good or ill,
To die, if needs be, doing their Lord's will.

Just then a satrap signals with raised arm,
And someone blows a horn with all his might,
At which the crowd with wide eyes, full of fright,
Drop flat upon their faces with alarm,
Cut down, upon the wailing of that horn,
Across the plain, like fallen stalks of corn.

Except for these young lads who stand their ground,
Resolved to bear clear witness to the truth,
Prepared to perish in the flower of youth,
Before they'll let the truth in lies be drowned.
They stand, assured the Author of all life
Can well sustain them in this hour of strife.

They stand, and by their standing, set men free;
They rip the shroud of darkness that has bound
Whole nations long since buried underground
In pagan fears, deprived of liberty.
Because God will be with them to the end,
These stand in faith, His fealty to defend!

Their lives, like three bright beacons, shine with light
Their beams point jointly upward to the skies,
To God, whose truth must triumph over lies,
Through brave hearts filled with courage, faith and love.
For God gives hope more glorious and secure,
Than that which any idol can procure.

The Battle of Glorieta Pass

by Brian Yapko

I'm old, my young ones. Soon I'll have to leave.
But ere we part I have just one tale more
To share—a tale of valor. Never grieve
A grandpa who helped win the Civil War!

Back then I was a farmer, country-born,
Ohio bred, blessed with an upright wife.
But once the South seceded I was sworn
To help preserve the Union with my life.

So Lincoln sent me to New Mexico,
A territory then—untamed and bold—
With Spanish ranches, cowboys, Navajo…
The trail to California's ports and gold.

Back East the War hit Shiloh and Bull Run.
Great generals led like Sherman, Grant and Lee.
New Mexico claims no such famous son—
Yet here the Union won its victory!

When Texan soldiers marched on Santa Fe
We Union troops marched south from Colorado.
Bullets flew between the Blue and Grey
And cannons rained down death with grim bravado.

We failed to see the Southern troops amass
And had to flee the field at deadly cost.
The rebel soldiers then attacked the Pass.
If Glorieta fell then all was lost!

Although our troops retreated in alarm
We vowed to keep the Territory free!
Outgunned, we met in stealth at Johnson's farm
And there devised our winning strategy:

A group of us slipped past the foe as spies
And gained advantage with this covert feat:
We found and then blew up the South's supplies!
The Texans had no choice but to retreat!

The War fought in the East was far from through.
But rebels never claimed the West again.
That was March of 1862—
A year that cost 200,000 men.

You say you love this country. Don't forget
We fought at Glorieta Pass for you—
Our lives and honor pledged to stop a threat
That tried to rip this sacred land in two!

So many valiant men have fought and died
Because we thought our country worth the fight.
The devil take the idiots who've lied
With claims this nation doesn't strive for right!

America's a land just like your mother—
Not quite unflawed but blest in her creation.
Where worth is based on work and nothing other—
The fairest way to build a righteous nation.

POET'S NOTE: The Battle of Glorieta Pass—frequently dubbed "the Gettysburg of the West"—was the decisive battle of the New Mexico campaign of the Civil War. It took place March 26-28, 1862. The Union victory put an end to Confederate dreams of taking California and the Southwest.

Canto 3: Ex-Wife

excerpted from The English Cantos Volume 2: StairWell

The Poet, with Dante and Virgil, has arrived on the third step of the StairWell, or Purgatory. Dante at the start of Canto 3 has been at pains to explain to the shocked Poet what just has happened on the second step. It has been an incredible, almost unbelievable encounter. Now they have forged forward and have had to fight through obstructions of ice. As finally, after considerable danger, they maneuver through, the Poet then encounters his ex-wife from over 40 years ago.

There, burnished with gold that her soul so prized,
The chair she sat on; and beside the gifts
That we'd exchanged in love, but she had seized.

Two rings, a bracelet—pure gold—other thefts
Of lesser value, and there the amulet,
Center of all, which left me most bereft:

Gold chain, with coffin figure, within set
Ivory inlaid to fill its key-like core;
Recalled to me what I'd tried to forget,

I turned to Dante, if he could help more?
Impassive, though, he stared straight through the queen,
Seated, quite unaware his presence there;

And Virgil—well—to him, what did it mean?
"I rule here," she said. "And here my writ runs,
For Midas grants me power which nothing screens:

One touch of mine is deadlier than a gun;
Flesh even turns to what I want, more gold!
Why—" Here she stood. "Once James, we two were fun;

But look now—you are poor, ha! You are old!
So let me touch, and ease your misery;
Your value I'll increase one hundred-fold!"

With that—her ominous first step towards me—
I tensed, treading backwards, in total fear,
My wretched mind revolving desperately—

Like some wasp buzzing in a locked jam jar,
Below it, perilous waters waiting patient—
And all I did not want looming so near.

The StairWell proving some deceptive agent
Delivering back to the Hell I had escaped
But lately. Indeed, some abortifacient—

For if I failed now, what would be my state?
Distracted by impending doom, I turned
Only to see the white ivory inlaid

Within the amulet, as in an urn,
Sacred, devoted, as some congealed ash
No fire destroyed, though thoroughly it burned.

Her hand reached out and with its merest brush
I too would be a brute inanimate,
And all my hopes for heaven helpless, crushed.

But in that space where time itself lacks state,
As neither forward nor backwards to go,
A knife-edge either way deciding fate,

So there I was, the amulet a-glow,
For why? What secret did ivory own—
Somehow to continue I had to know.

"Hari," I blurted, "ivory's real bone:
That child we had together, you destroyed,
His flesh and blood consumed, and his soul's gone

To heaven!" I cried to God. "My dear boy!"
No more her peril vexed me or her touch—
Something had been lost money couldn't buy,

Or all the gold she'd stored in her greed's pouch.
And she—as ivory preoccupied
My mind—too felt its memory, and blanched,

Stalled in her tracks, remembered her boy, dead;
One she'd forced down and out her crotch's chute.
"I don't care, I don't care," she said, and lied.

For now, some tear—but one as black as soot—
Tried forming in the corner of her eye,
But finding release from her flesh, could not.

Held back, held onto, so how could she cry?
Where was release? Within, a speck before
Not visible, now half-crawled out, a fly

Lodged on her duct, so well fed, dripping spores,
Bloated, and like its mistress, simply stuck
There: far too fat to leave, effect a cure.

And yet, half out this way, wriggling—a crack
Appeared in her countenance, an askew
Eye saw the fly and memory brought back

The clinic—killing—and the wrong she knew
She'd done—dead child of whom I only dream,
How in my heart my being longs for you!

Yet, yet … she took your life before your name
Was ever called—who are you? And what be?
See us, me too, this golden waste of shame

Around—deserts of her idolatry!
But she, constricted, choked and rendered dumb,
Could hardly move, much less attack, touch me.

That fatal moment when God's judgement comes,
Which every human gets to at some point,
Deciding whether they go up, slip down,

And now, her eye blotted as by black paint,
Disfigured as its fly expanded forth,
She turned, staggered as one about to faint,

But holding up until she felt support—
Grasping the amulet, pressing in my hand,
Rendering back to me our dead child's worth

In ivory. And as she did I understood
Or thought I did—she now hysterical,
Yet silent as a block of hardest wood

For nothing could come out, compressed withal;
We both may, shocked, have stayed there till doom's day;
But short steps to the edge, that was all,

As Dante herded, bid us not delay;
The desert-ocean had its golden shore,
A precipice on which last outcomes played.

But what she did next, why, I wasn't sure:
Collapsing down as Crassus did, his throat
To be the moat on which the Parthians poured

Gold loved so much by him. Another note,
However, sounded as of some release:
A flapping, light, as if about to float,

And not that hostile buzzing of disease
Infecting her eye; I looked, and there, red
Which black before, was struggling but to seize

Its living back, which for so long had fled;
So now in metamorphosis red changed,
First black to red and then even that bled

Away. At last, all had to be expunged.
Around my knees she clung, began to wail,
Her very eyes—liquefying squeezed sponges—

If that her tears so long held in her soul
Might finally be free—but fluttering,
I saw it, heard a new voice say it all:

The fly—no longer one—now took to wing,
A butterfly so beautiful, so light,
So graceful, its sight induced in me song—

Charged and transported—I'd made paradise,
At least in that moment. I wondered hard
To see it soar so fragile, free in flight,

But more still—a wonder I preferred:
Below, gold altered so, its dust to brown
With shoots of green, as if the conscience stirred

Meant earth returned, reclaimed its own,
And what was dead might incredibly live
Through Him whose dying, death couldn't keep down.

Quiet, she stood beside me now. "Forgive,"
At last, she said, and what else could I do?
"With all my heart," I said, "But I must leave."

But now beside us, stood Dante, Virgil too,
Standing as if awaiting some last act
Which I'd commission though what, I didn't know.

Ahead, the ground her butterfly had raked
With aerial beauty, now seemed fertile soil,
Living and moist, half solid and half lake.

My palm felt warm: in it, about to sail,
I felt the amulet expanding fast
Eager to launch and be free of its jail.

I knew then what to do: one motion cast
The gold away and ivory in it.
See, how it flashed in flight, and fell at last

Into the lake-land's alive, living pit,
Wherein, not sinking, but like a small boat
Held up, and following with innate wit

Her butterfly on its long, distant float.
How tiny—ivory in such a big sea,
But even so it seemed bigger, full of hope:

Indeed, as I strained my eyes, tried to see
More, yes, becoming clear, expanding, there
The gold dissolving, but not ivory—

I saw its shape take form, taking in air,
Enlarging as if new breathing began—
And in my heart of hearts I found a prayer,

A blessing: I was seeing my lost son,
Whom she had killed, adrift, and in pursuit
Of where his mother's butterfly would land.

I waved—like some lost soul's desperate salute;
Perhaps his eyes were formed and he'd respond—
Or lips cry, "Father"! But his lips were mute.

As slowly the ivory confined went beyond
My vision, I felt my being shut down,
Go quiet, struggling so to understand—

My breath to hardly breathe, or heart to pound.
Yet all the while, as sight became a speck
On the cruel world's vast and receding round,

I saw the body form: its head from neck,
Limbs shaping outwards in perfect legs, arms;
I sensed his blood even, suffuse his cheeks;

And as I did my inner self went calm.
I turned, full knowing I'd not see again
My precious boy; yet now what was, was balm.

Heroic child, though you were never born,
Like Herakles to the furthest western point
To find Hesperides, fearless you'd gone;

Over the horizon's edge, the while each joint
Of you reformed itself into the one
I call, "My son." You did not disappoint.

She stood there, still crying, tears still not done;
Till Dante touched her shoulder—so light, deft,
I'm sure she barely felt; but change came on,

As nakedness is altered once it's dressed,
As if the honey of his hands allowed
Her emptiness to have some sweetness left.

"Hari," I said, "You've cried. I too broke vows;
And now our boy flies to the Western Isles
Whom we may never see just once—God knows

His living eyes. So let us without guile
Forgive; commit to love our other child;
At last then—" here I choked—"end this turmoil:

Conclude today what our mad years made wild."
She stood, she looked for all the world as lost,
Drained—majesty void, divested, and grown old;

Who'd think to grow so rich might end a cost?
Had even Dante's touch restored her soul?
I sensed beside me Virgil anxious most

To move on—we could not let Hari stall
Our progress: other levels beckoned near,
Already time ran out. I felt the pull

Ahead. "Hari, listen—we've lost what's dear—
Almost ourselves as well in what we did;
I must go, climb further and leave you here,

But you must not permit your pain be hid,
Returning to those sterile, golden shores,
Pretending Midas can be your true god.

Your butterfly's exposed that god's lush flaws;
Gird yourself, and prepare to follow him
When grieving's done and ego's emptied, poor.

She stirred then—tremulous, a sort of whimper.
Finally, "Why bring me out of the womb?
Why not be dead before I have a name?

Why live where I can never be at home?
Why knees receive me and why breasts to nurse?
Why not in darkness stay than living roam?

Perish the day my father blessed my birth
And said, 'O joy, to us a daughter's born.
No, rather, begetting, let him be cursed.'

With that she stopped, and teetered over, swooned.
I caught her just in time. With Virgil's help
We laid her where fresh lilies lately grown

Adorned a bank of solid earth, not pelf,
All that was gone—a new world dawned; and she—
A beauty sleeping there—might come to health

Once some angelic prince, but never me,
Arrived and with one kiss her soul would start.
But we'd no time to dither, destiny

Must run its course. To see her broke my heart
Thus on the ground. But Dante urged the way
Before, and going meant we'd shed the hurt.

So, one last time, I knelt just where she laid
And gently kissed her forehead, and said, "less."
At last some sort of peace between us made.

Not looking back, but that last tenderness
I treasured in my soul and more beside—
Where had he flown—my son—I could not guess?

Onward, both Dante, Virgil with huge strides
Pressed forward, as if leaving me behind,
So dilatory I, and now the gulf so wide;

I ran as one possessed, or out of mind,
To catch them up, when round a sudden bend
They disappeared, so ominous a sign:

To lose my mentors and come to this end—
How would I fare without their wisdom, love?
I raced with all the strength I had to mend

How far apart we were—and reached the curve
Where they'd gone round, but as I did stopped short,
Amazed—before my eyes, rising above

The whole landscape, stood a bridge, metal, taut,
All shiny, surface smooth as polished steel—
Far side a building, political, fraught

With all of thinking's miscegenated ills:
A school, to wit, where education deals.

VII. TRANSLATIONS

Books and Butterflies 4 by Steven J. Levin, 2017, oil on canvas, 36 x 24 in, private collection. (stevenjlevin.com)

悼亡

天上星河轉 Tiānshàng xīnghé zhuǎn
人間簾幕垂 Rénjiān lián mù chuí
涼生枕簟淚痕滋 Liáng shēng zhěn diàn lèihén zī
起解羅衣聊問 Qǐ jiè luó yī liáo wèn
夜何其 Yè héqí

翠貼蓮蓬小 Cuì tiē liánpeng xiǎo
金銷藕葉稀 Jīn xiāo ǒu yè xī
舊時天氣舊時衣 Jiù shí tiānqì jiù shí yī
只有情懷不似 Zhǐyǒu qíng huái bù shì
舊家時 Jiù jiā shí

Mourning the Dead

by Li Qingzhao, Southern Song (1084-1155)
translated by Talbot Hook

Above in the heavens the star-river flows;
Down on the earth the curtains hang low.
As the air grows chill, and my pillow tear-damp,
I arise, untying my robes just to know
The hours the night has tolled.

The patched emerald lotus of my robe is frayed;
Its gold-gilded leaves of late seem to fade.
Same is the weather, and same are my clothes—
It's only my feelings that seem to have strayed
From our home-times of old.

NOTE: This poem was likely written sometime after the death of her husband in 1129 as they fled south after the Jurchen invasion of northern China. 星河 (xīnghé), literally "star-river", is one of several terms for the Milky Way.

竹 里 館

獨 坐 幽 篁 裡, Dú zuò yōu huáng lǐ
彈 琴 復 長 嘯. Tánqín fù chángxiào
深 林 人 不 知, Shēnlín rén bùzhī
明 月 來 相 照. Míng yuè lái xiāng zhào

Bamboo-Grove Pavilion

by Wang Wei (699-759)
translated by Talbot Hook

Seated alone in a dim bamboo grove,
Plucking the strings and humming a song —
Deep in the forest and unknown to men,
The glistening moon comes gleaming along.

Ballade

Las! Mort, qui t'a fait si hardie,
De prendre la noble princesse
Qui estoit mon confort, ma vie,
Mon bien, mon plaisir, ma richesse!
Puis que tu as prins ma maistresse,
Prens moi aussi, son serviteur,
Car j'ayme mieulx prouchainement
Mourir que languir en tourment,
En paine, soussi et douleur.

Las! De tous biens estoit garnie
Et en droite fleur de jeunesse!
Je pry à Dieu qu'il te maudie,
Faulse Mort, plaine de rudesse!
Se prise l'eusses en vieillesse,
Ce ne fust pas si grant rigueur,
Mais prise l'a hastivement,
Et m'a laissié piteusement
En paine, soussi et douleur.

Las! Je suis seul, sans compaignie.
Adieu, ma Dame, ma liesse!
Or est nostre amour departie;
Non pour tant, je vous fais promesse
Que de prieres, à largesse,
Morte vous serviray de cueur,
Sans oublier aucunement,
E vous regretteray souvent,
En paine, soussi et douleur.

Ballade for His Lady Deceased

by Charles d'Orléans (1394–1465)
translated by Margaret Coats

Alas, Death, who made you so bold?
My noble princess you possess;
My life and comfort you enfold,
My pleasure, wealth, and cheerfulness.
Since you my mistress now oppress,
Take me, her servant since we met,
For I would soon die willingly
Instead of living mournfully
In pain, affliction, and regret.

Alas for merit placed to mold
In modest bloom of youthfulness!
I beg, my God, swallow up cold
Brutish Death so pitiless.
Had she reached age's helplessness,
Such sorrow it would not beget,
But she was seized too hastily,
And I am left pathetically
In pain, affliction, and regret.

Alas! I bide here unconsoled.
Lady, adieu, my happiness!
Now for our love the bell has tolled,
But for your soul I make redress
With alms and fasts and prayerfulness.
Though you are dead, I serve you yet,
For I have loved you loyally,
And think of you repeatedly,
In pain, affliction, and regret.

(continued)

Dieu, sur tout souverain Seigneur,
Ordonnez, par grace et doulceur,
De l'ame d'elle, tellement
Qu'elle ne soit pas longuement
En paine, soussi et douleur.

O God, above all sovereigns set,
Command that by your grace her debt
For lapses be paid speedily;
May she not linger wearily
In pain, affliction, and regret.

TRANSLATOR'S NOTE: This poem may be about Bonne d'Armagnac, the second wife of Charles d'Orléans. The current Wikipedia article on Charles says erroneously that Bonne was divorced. Rather, Charles was taken prisoner by the victorious English at the Battle of Agincourt, and as a royal prince, held hostage in England for 25 years. During this time Bonne's father was leader of the Orléans party in France (which became known as the Armagnac party). Bonne died 15 or 20 years after Charles was captured. The poem may, however, refer to an Englishwoman whom Charles came to love. Her identity is uncertain; she was probably the wife of a nobleman charged with the custody of the royal hostage. This lady too died before the English accepted a ransom to return the much-distraught Charles to France.

Poet Basho and Moon Festival by Tsukioka Yoshitoshi, 1891, ukiyo-e woodblock print. Poet Matsuo Basho meets with two farmers who celebrate the mid-autumn Moon Festival. A haiku adorns it.

Summer Grasses

This is one of Basho's most celebrated haiku, composed in tears while visiting the site where Minamoto Yoshitsune (1159–1189) had lived, but where no building remained.

by Matsuo Basho (1644-1694),
translated by Margaret Coats

Summer grasses grow
Where noblest ancient warriors
Laid their heads to dream.

Natsukusa ya
tsuwamono-domo ga
yume no ato.

Regenlied

Walle, Regen, walle nieder,
Wecke mir die Träume wieder,
Die ich in der Kindheit träumte,
Wenn das Naß im Sande schäumte!

Wenn die matte Sommerschwüle
Lässig stritt mit frischer Kühle,
Und die blanken Blätter tauten,
Und die Saaten dunkler blauten.

Welche Wonne, in dem Fließen
Dann zu stehn mit nackten Füßen,
An dem Grase hin zu streifen
Und den Schaum mit Händen greifen,

Oder mit den heißen Wangen
Kalte Tropfen aufzufangen,
Und den neuerwachten Düften
Seine Kinderbrust zu lüften!

Wie die Kelche, die da troffen,
Stand die Seele atmend offen,
Wie die Blumen, düftetrunken,
In dem Himmelstau versunken.

Schauernd kühlte jeder Tropfen
Tief bis an des Herzens Klopfen,
Und der Schöpfung heilig Weben
Drang bis ins verborgne Leben.

Rain Song

by Klaus Groth (1819-1899)
translated by Julian Woodruff

Pour, O rain, pour down to earth,
Give my childhood dreams rebirth,
When in reverie I roamed
Shores where sand with moisture foamed.

When the summer sun's hot rays
Idly vied with crisper days,
And the pale leaves dripped with dew,
And seeds sprouted darkest blue.

What bliss then when surf would greet
Bare and eager waiting feet!
Grass that grew for sweep of sole,
Hands for snatching foam from shoal;

Or else on those burning cheeks
Catch the cooling rainy streaks,
And to every new-borne scent
See that youthful breast was lent.

Like the chalices that dripped.
Freely breathed the soul and sipped,
Like the flowers with fragrance drunk,
In the dew from heaven sunk.

Shudd'ring did each drop impart
Cooling deep within my heart,
And the web creation wove
Toward my inmost essence strove.

(continued)

Walle, Regen, walle nieder,
Wecke meine alten Lieder,
Die wir in der Türe sangen,
Wenn die Tropfen draußen klangen!

Möchte ihnen wieder lauschen,
Ihrem süßen, feuchten Rauschen,
Meine Seele sanft betauen
Mit dem frommen Kindergrauen.

Pour, O rain, pour down to earth,
Reawaken songs of mirth
And of gladness that we sang
When without the raindrops rang!

Murmuring so sweet and moist,
If I heard I would rejoice,
And my soul softly bedew
With the awe my childhood knew.

Canzoniere del Petrarca 359

Quando il soave mio fido conforto
per dar riposo a la mia vita stanca
ponsi del letto in su la sponda manca
con quel suo dolce ragionare accorto,
tutto di pièta et di paura smorto
dico, "Onde vien tu ora, o felice alma?"
Un ramoscel di palma
et un di lauro trae del suo bel seno,
et dice, "Dal sereno
Ciel empireo et di quelle sante parti
mi mossi, et vengo sol per consolarti."

In atto et in parole la ringrazio
umilemente, et poi demando, "Or donde
sai tu il mio stato?" Et ella, "Le triste onde
del pianto di che mai tu non se' sazio,
coll'aura de' sospir', per tanto spazio
passano al Cielo et turban la mia pace.
Si forte ti dispiace
che di questa miseria sia partita
et giunta a miglior vita?
Che piacer ti devria, se tu m'amasti
quanto in sembianti et ne' tuoi dir mostrasti.

Canzone on a Dream of Laura

by Francesco Petrarch (1304-1374)
translated by Margaret Coats

When softly my sustaining comfort stirs
Herself to offer solace coveted,
Advancing toward the left side of my bed
With that sweet courtly reasoning of hers,
In fearful homage all my being murmurs,
"O happy soul, from what sphere do you come?"
    A little frond of palm, and some
Fresh laurel she draws outward to be seen,
    Whispering, "From the pure serene
Far Heaven empyrean do I proceed,
To bring you consolation in your need."

With humble words and gestures I express
My thanks, and wonder how she knows my plight.
"Your sighs and ceaseless weeping storm the height
Of Heaven, and render my peace there the less,"
She says. "Does it cause you such distress
That I have left this misery behind,
    The very best of bliss to find?
It should please you, if you love me so well
    As when you ventured to excel
All lovers with your tender, plaintive looks,
And poets who composed most ardent books."

(continued)

Rispondo, "Io non piango altro che me stesso
che son rimaso in tenebre e 'n martire,
certo sempre del tuo al Ciel salire
come di cosa ch' uom vede da presso.
Come Dio et Natura avrebben messo
in un cor giovenil tanta vertute,
se l'eterna salute
non fusse destinata al tuo ben fare?
O de l'anime rare
ch' altamente vivesti qui tra noi
et che subito al Ciel volasti poi."

"Ma io che debbo altro che pianger sempre
misero et sol, che senza te son nulla.
Ch' or fuss' io spento al latte et a la culla,
per non provar de l'amorose tempre."
Et ella, "A che pur piangi et ti distempre?
Quanto era meglio alzar da terra l'ali,
et le cose mortali
et queste dolci tue fallaci ciance
librar con giusta lance,
et seguire me (s' è ver che tanto m'ami),
cogliendo omai qualcun di questi rami."

"I' volea demandar," respond' io allora,
"che voglion importar quelle due frondi?"
Et ella, "Tu medesmo ti rispondi,
tu la cui penna tanto l'una onora.
Palma è vittoria, et io giovene ancora
vinsi il mondo et me stessa; il lauro segna
triunfo, ond' io son degna
mercé di quel Signor che mi die' forza.
Or tu, s' altri ti sforza,
a lui ti svolgi, a lui chiedi soccorso
sí che siam seco al fine del tuo corso."

"I weep for nothing," I respond, "except
Myself, here yet in shadows and in pain,
For you are Heaven's prize, I ascertain,
As sure as if I saw you there upswept.
Why would Nature and God form you adept
Beyond your peers in virtue's cultivation,
    Unless assuredly salvation
Were destined your reward for holy deeds?
    O rare soul whom the Spirit leads,
You are one who, with us, would live on high,
And when released, to Heaven at once could fly."

"Do not," I go on, "my restlessness impugn;
Sore solitude produces only weeping.
Would I had perished as an infant sleeping
New cradled, from Love's bitter trials immune."
"Tears," she rejoins, "your melodies untune.
Much better had it been to raise your wings
    And rightly gaze at mortal things,
Including those sweet fallacies of yours,
    For if the love your verse outpours
For me be true, you should make good your vows,
And gather at least one of these fair boughs."

"Tell me what leaves from those two twigs are sprung,"
I plead, "I weep because I yearn to ask."
"Your pen," she states, "ought to take up that task,
Since you to honor one so much have sung.
The palm is victory, for though still young,
Myself and the world I quelled; this labor's laurel
    Marks my triumph earned by moral
Conduct, thanks to the Lord who gave me strength.
    If other leaders rule your length
Of years, turn now to make my Lord your friend,
That we may be together at your end."

(continued)

"Son questi i capei biondi et l'aureo nodo,"
dich' io, "ch' ancor mi stringe, et quei belli occhi
che fur mio sol?" "Non errar con li sciocchi,
né parlar," dice, "o creder a lor modo.
Spirito ignudo sono e 'n Ciel mi godo;
quel che tu cerchi è terra già molt' anni.
Ma per trarti d'affanni
m'è dato a parer tale, et ancor quella
sarò più che mai bella,
a te più cara, sì selvaggia et pia,
salvando inseme tua salute et mia."

I' piango; et ella il volto
co le sue man m'asciuga, et poi sospira
dolcemente, et s'adira
con parole che i sassi romper ponno;
et dopo questo si parte ella e 'l sonno.

"Is this gold hair the knot that yet results
In my constraint? And are these eyes my sun?"
I cry, and she replies, "At last have done
With words like those of fools in erring cults.
I am an unclothed spirit who exults
In Heaven; what you seek has long been earth.
   But bringing you true balm of worth,
I stand here now as ever I shall be,
   More beautiful in charity,
No longer wild, kinder than you have known,
Safeguarding your salvation and my own."

   I weep; she dries my tearful face
Gently with her hands, and sighs with great
   Affection, but then becomes irate
In speech that could break boulders by its arts,
And after, with my sleep, she departs.

TRANSLATOR'S NOTE: Italian poet Francesco Petrarca (1304–1374) carefully created a sequence of 366 poems, mostly sonnets, telling of his love for Laura, a Provençal lady. The story and the poet's work cover many years, from the day he met Laura in 1327, to long after her demise in the first wave of the Black Death (1348). In poems before the pivotal event of the lady's death, Petrarch as lover hears her voice only as enchanting music. This poem near the very end of the collection is the only one in which a meaningful dialogue takes place. In form, it is a canzone or "long song" with unique shape. Petrarch's work was the single most important influence on European love poetry for 300 years after his death.

Pasqua!

A che l'amaro strazio sulla croce,
O martire del Golgota, se'l mondo
Sul cui versasti il sangue è si feroce
E l'uomo del peccato non è mondo?!

Se l'hai redento e tratto dell'atroce
Mal di lebbra e del servile pondo,
Perchè dal brutto istinto e l'impudore,
Neglettamente, non lavaste il core?

Oggi è Pasqua, e dal sepolcro oscuro
Al ciel risale con spedito passo
Con squil di tromb' e rullo di tamburro.

Ma quella terra che tu lasc' in basso
Rest' al governo parzial' e impuro
Dello stesso Pilato e Caifasso.

Easter!

by Rosario Previti (1882-1967)
translated by Joseph S. Salemi

Why your bitter torment on the cross,
Martyr of Golgotha, if the world on which
You poured your blood in agony remains
Savage and fierce, and man still steeped in sin?

The hand that healed the leprous and the lame
Did not cleanse the craving, evil heart—
Why not wash away its shamelessness,
Its brutal instincts and ferocity?

Today is Easter—from the tomb's cold dark
You climb again to heaven with quick steps,
To trumpet-flourish and the roll of drums.

But that same earth which you leave behind
Rests in the tainted, bought, and weighted hands
Of Caiaphas and Pilate, and their spawn.

POET'S NOTE: This is a poem by my grandfather, from his book *Raccolta di Poesie Siciliane e Italiane* (Messina: Edizioni Ferrara, 1960). He was an anarchist, a Deist, and a Freemason, and a very intense anticlerical. The poem is in standard Italian hendecasyllables, with the rhyme scheme ABABABCCDEDEDE. I have translated without rhyme, in order to maintain closeness with the poem's meaning.

Einsamkeit

Wie eine trübe Wolke
Durch heitre Lüfte geht,
Wenn in der Tanne Wipfel
Ein mattes Lüftchen weht:

So zieh' ich meine Straße
Dahin mit trägem Fuß,
Durch helles, frohes Leben,
Einsam und ohne Gruß.

Ach, dass die Luft so ruhig!
Ach, dass die Welt so licht!
Als noch die Stürme tobten,
War ich so elend nicht.

Solitude

by Wilhelm Müller (1794-1827)
translated by Joseph Greene

As when a cloud is darkened
And drifts through sunlit sky,
While through the many treetops
An icy breeze does fly:

As such I make my journey
I trek with weary feet,
All round me life is cheerful,
But I've no friends to greet.

Alas, the air's so peaceful!
Alas, the world's so bright!
When storms would rage and thunder,
My torment had less bite.

Ständchen

Leise flehen meine Lieder
Durch die Nacht zu Dir;
In den stillen Hain hernieder,
Liebchen, komm' zu mir!

Flüsternd schlanke Wipfel rauschen
In des Mondes Licht;
Des Verräters feindlich Lauschen
Fürchte, Holde, nicht.

Hörst die Nachtigallen schlagen?
Ach! sie flehen Dich,
Mit der Töne süßen Klagen
Flehen sie für mich.

Sie verstehn des Busens Sehnen,
Kennen Liebesschmerz,
Rühren mit den Silbertönen
Jedes weiche Herz.

Lass auch Dir die Brust bewegen,
Liebchen, höre mich!
Bebend harr' ich Dir entgegen!
Komm', beglücke mich!

Serenade

by Ludwig Rellstab (1799-1860)
  translated by Joseph Greene

Lightly singing, softly pleading
Through the night to thee;
In the silent grove proceeding,
Dearest, come to me!

Slender treetops gently swaying
In the soft moonlight;
Of the bitter fiend betraying
Dear, be not affright.

Nightingales are sweetly singing
Ah! They beg of thee,
With their pleading music ringing
They implore for me.

They have known the inner yearning,
Known the lover's grief,
Now their melodies returning
Bring the heart relief.

Let thy heart be moved to passion,
Dearest, hear my plea!
Trembling I await my dear one!
Come bring peace to me!

Herbstbild

Dieß ist ein Herbsttag, wie ich keinen sah!
Die Luft ist still, als athmete man kaum,
Und dennoch fallen raschelnd, fern und nah,
Die schönsten Früchte ab von jedem Baum.
O stört sie nicht, die Feier der Natur!
Dieß ist die Lese, die sie selber hält,
Denn heute lös't sich von den Zweigen nur,
Was vor dem milden Strahl der Sonne fällt.

Spring

by Friedrich Hebbel
translated by Sean Thompson

A spring as fine as this I can't recall!
No wandering breath of wind disturbs the air,
Yet still is heard the gentle rustling fall
Of ripest fruit from branches here and there.
Disturb it not, this, Nature's sacred rite!
This is the harvest that is self-performed,
The sun alone, with mild and kindly light,
Can lift the fruit from off the trees, soft-warmed.

П. Чайковскому

К отъезду музыканта-друга
Мой стих минорный тон берет,
И нашей старой дружбы фуга,
Все развиваяся, растет…

Мы увертюру жизни бурной
Сыграли вместе до конца,
Грядущей славы марш бравурный
Нам рано волновал сердца;

В свои мы верили таланты,
Делились массой чувств, идей…
И был ты вроде доминанты
В аккордах юности моей.

Увы, та песня отзвучала,
Иным я звукам отдался,
Я детонировал немало
И с диссонансами сжился;

Давно без счастья и без дела
Дары небес я растерял
Мне жизнь, как гамма, надоела,
И близок, близок мой финал…

Но ты — когда для жизни вечной
Меня зароют под землей, —
Ты в нотах памяти сердечной
Не ставь бекара предо мной.
1893 г.

To Tchaikovsky

by A.N. Apukhtin (1840-1893)
translated by Olga Dumer

With my musician friend's departure
A minor key pervades my lines.
Yet, like a fugue's evolving texture,
Old friendship amplifies with time.

We played together, with bravura,
Our youthful daring prelude.
Since adolescence, fame's allure
Thrilled our hearts with festive mood.

And we had faith in our flair,
We shared our feelings and beliefs…
Within the score of my young years
Yours was the leading leitmotif.

Alas! That melody once faded,
Another tune took hold of me,
My sense of harmony abated
And often I would sing off key.

My life without aim or fortune
Like tedious scales, is dull and bland.
God-given talent hasn't flourished,
And my finale is near at hand.

But when the time comes for my burial
And I transcend to the Divine—
Please in the chords of your memorial
Don't mark me with a natural sign.

El Arpa

Del salón en el ángulo oscuro,
de su dueña tal vez olvidada,
silenciosa y cubierta de polvo
veíase el arpa.

¡Cuánta nota dormía en sus cuerdas,
como el pájaro duerme en las ramas,
esperando la mano de nieve,
que sabe arrancarlas!

¡Ay!—pensé; cuántas veces el genio
así duerme en el fondo del alma!
y una voz, como Lázaro, espera
que le diga: "¡Levántate y anda!"

The Harp

by Gustavo Bécquer
translated by Cheryl Corey

Obscured by corner shadows, gathering dust, perhaps
forgotten over time—there stands the silent harp.

So many hidden notes entombed on muted strings,
which like a bird asleep upon a steadfast bough,
await the snow-white hand who makes their music sing.

Alas! So too, I've often thought, the spirit sleeps.
It waits, like Lazarus, deep within the soul, until
it hears a voice—the Lord's command: "Arise and walk!"

Les Deux Cortèges

Deux cortèges se sont rencontrés à l'église.
L'un est morne : — il conduit le cercueil d'un enfant ;
Une femme le suit, presque folle, étouffant
Dans sa poitrine en feu le sanglot qui la brise.

L'autre, c'est un baptême ! — au bras qui le défend
Un nourrisson gazouille une note indécise ;
Sa mère, lui tendant le doux sein qu'il épuise,
L'embrasse tout entier d'un regard triomphant !

On baptise, on absout, et le temple se vide.
Les deux femmes, alors, se croisant sous l'abside,
Échangent un coup d'œil aussitôt détourné ;
Et — merveilleux retour qu'inspire la prière —
La jeune mère pleure en regardant la bière,
La femme qui pleurait sourit au nouveau-né !

The Two Corteges

by Joséphin Soulary (1815-1891)
translated by Hadyn Adams

Within a church two groups of people met:
An infant's funeral cortege, the first:
A woman followed, her heart fit to burst
Within her breast repressing her regret.

The second for a baptism all set;
The mother her young baby gently nursed
Within her cradling arms as she rehearsed
A smile of pleasure she would never forget.

Then these two women brief glances exchanged
As the church emptied, the services complete.
It seemed therein a miracle arranged
As their paths crossed whilst making their retreat:
For, seeing the coffin, the young mother grieved,
While the baby the other's tears relieved.

Un Fiore

A Giannina Milli

Fragil erba questo fiore
Di mia mano un dì piantai:
Io di nuovo fresco umore
Le sue barbe alimentai:
Per me nacque, per me crebbe,
Per me vita il fiore s'ebbe.
Jeri il sole tramontava,
E col raggio suo morente
La virtute a me mancava,
S'offuscava la mia mente;
Mi sentiva oltre l'usato
Dentro l'anima affannato.
Qui nel petto mi batteva
Una febbre irrequieta;
Io con ansia m'inchiedeva
Dove fosse la mia meta,
Dove un'anima io trovassi,
In cui l'alma io riposassi.
E tra l'ombre del pensiere
Alla nera fantasia,
Come stella in cielo nero,
Un sembiante m'apparia,
Dal cui sguardo rilucente
Tutta io bevvi un'alma ardente.
Chiedi, o donna, alla tua lira
I più armonici concenti;
Chiedi al genio, che t'ispira,
Chiedi i sogni più ridenti:
Forse esprimer tu potrai
Quel che in seno allor provai.
Io recisi il fiore allor,
E ti porto, o donna, il fior.

A Flower

for Giannina Milli

by Alceste De Lollis (1820-1887)
translated by Adam Sedia

A fragile herb, this blooming flower,
I planted with my hand one day;
Once more I fed refreshing power
Into its bristling barbs' array;
  By me it sprung, by me it grew,
  By me it had the life it drew.

Just yesterday the sun was setting
And fast upon its dying ray
The virtue that I was forgetting
Darkened my mind gone far astray;
  I withered as my senses stole
  Away from my tormented soul.

A relentless fever was beating
Here within my restless chest;
I anxiously began entreating
Where my life's path should come to rest,
  Where I could find a soul so close
  That in it my soul could repose.

And through the shadows of my thought
Unto the blackest fantasy,
Like stars with which black night is fraught,
A ghostly form appeared to me,
  From whose far-shining, lucid gaze
  I glimpsed another soul ablaze.

(continued)

Se di giorni non ingrati,
Se di gioja non mentita,
Se d'istanti fortunati
Non fia scarsa a te la vita;
Quando un labile momento
Potrai coglier di contento,
Godi, o donna, godi allor;
Non pensare a questo fior.
A 'tuo' piedi versi il mondo
I suoi doni, i suoi tesori;
Ti sia sempre il ciel secondo,
Ti ricinga di splendori.
Quando in core esulterai,
E la gloria gusterai,
Non pensare, o donna, allor,
Non pensar a questo fior.
Ma nell'ore tue secrete,
Ma ne'taciti momenti,
Quando in cerca di quiete,
Spaventata a' di fuggenti,
Sentirai l'alma dimessa
Ricader sovra sè stessa;
Ti ricordi, o donna, al cor,
Ti ricordi del mio fior.
E se un'onda allor d'affetto
Con affanno sollevata
Cercherà fuori del petto
Alla vita desolata
Sola un'alma che t'intenda,
Ti penetri, ti comprenda . . .
Premi o donna, premi allor
Questo fiore sopra il cor.

— 10 Agosto 1850

Ask, then, O lady, ask your lyre
To sound its sweetest harmonies;
Ask for your genius to inspire,
Ask for the visions that most please:
Perhaps at last you could express
What I held fast within my breast.
  I cut the flower to be true,
    And bring it, O lady, to you.

If days that pass without regret,
If joy not feigned or counterfeit,
If moments you count fortunate
Remain to you, not yet forfeit;
If in a fleeting moment's bliss
You capture some small happiness,
  Rejoice, O lady, then rejoice;
    Give this flower no thought or voice.

But in your hours of solitude,
In moments when deep silence weighs,
When surrounded by quietude,
Terrified at the fleeing days,
You feel your soul collapse, resigned,
Upon itself, upon your mind;
  Recall, O lady, in your heart,
    Recall the flower I impart.

And if, once care has been suppressed,
A drowning wave of pure sensation
Searches outside the trembling breast
Into the life of desolation,
One soul alone will dare attend you,
One soul alone will comprehend you . . .
  Take, O lady, before I part;
    Take this flower upon your heart.

The Poet's Spirit

To the Memory of Alceste De Lollis

Alceste De Lollis (1820-1887) was a minor poet of risorgimento-era Abruzzo. The translator's grandmother, Anne Sedia (née De Lollis) was the great-granddaughter of the poet's double cousin. The family claims to descend from Marcus Lollius Paulinus (c. 55-2 BC), to whom, along with his son Publius Lollius Maximus, Horace addressed several poems (Odes 4.9, 34-44; Epistles 1.2, 18). The poem translated was the only work of De Lollis that the translator could locate, and he would appreciate any assistance in discovering more works.

by Adam Sedia

> Across two centuries' and an ocean's span,
> You born to Dante's, I to Shakespeare's tongue,
> Our blood unites us, scions of one clan,
> Whose forebears Horace entertained in song.
> But more than blood spans distance, tongue, and time:
> The flame, the spirit that all poets share—
> The ear attuned to music, rhythm, and rhyme;
> The eye aware of beauty everywhere
> And in it Truth, eternal, changeless, clear;
> The mind that can extract the hidden good.
> These unseen bonds of spirit draw us near—
> More than mere blood and surname ever could.
> Though blood will perish, spirit never dies,
> And thus is where our truest kinship lies.

VIII. ESSAYS

Young Girl Reading by Jean Honoré Fragonard, 1770-1772, oil on canvas, 32.2 x 25.5 in.

Poetic Pitfalls

by Joseph S. Salemi

There are a number of ways to go wrong in poetry. Unfortunately, the Poetry Establishment is only willing to admit the existence of a select few of them. The others are either kept under wraps or disguised as acceptable options.

Let's start with the common errors—that is, the ones that all the mainstream teachers and workshop jockeys agree upon, and which are therefore well known to pretty much everybody. These errors are lambasted and ridiculed so often that they are tatterdemalion scarecrows, universally familiar. Here goes:

1. *Using too many words when fewer would suffice.* In general, yes, this is an error. Concision and pithiness are in most cases preferable to long-winded blather. Don't be a Polonius.

2. *Being overly dependent on adjectives.* You can pull off multi-adjectival usage if you're in the league of Francis Thompson, but in most other poets it's a sign of self-indulgence and showiness.

3. *Editorializing in an open and blatant manner.* Unless you're writing hard satire, this is to be avoided. It's common sense not to be an earnest poltroon, straightforwardly orating to one's readers.

4. *Depending on abstract nouns rather than concrete images.* As a rule of thumb, there's little to argue with here. Too many abstractions swathe a poem in vagueness, and hamper the reader's ability to visualize your language.

5. *Employing extremely old-fashioned diction.* Again, who could disagree? Using eftsoons, aught, methinks, or the older hath and doth conjugations is probably over the top.

The strictures against these errors are sort of like the rules for proper behavior in a playground. They are practical guidelines, not divine decrees. Exceptions can and do occur to every one of them. But if you consider the five "errors" as a whole, a very interesting picture of mainstream poetic expectations emerges. Avoiding them is really about maintaining loyalty to two contradictory things: immediacy and indirection.

On the one hand they reject rhetoric, abstract language, and archaism as obstacles between the poet and the reader; and on the other hand they call for a reticence and a crypticism that hesitate to come right out and say something. In short, they represent the quandary of classic modernism: How can we have the robust earthiness of Robert Browning within the chaste confines of Hilda Doolittle?

It can't be done, of course, but that has never stopped partisans from adhering to an ideal. The entire modernist enterprise in poetry has been an attempt to square the circle, so to speak. Modernism wanted a poetry that hits you like an endorphin rush, but that also shrouds itself in crypticism and mystery. It asks that we be mightily moved by that which is small and obscure.

In fact, you might even boil down modernist aesthetics in poetry to the following recipe. Let's title it "How To Write A Modernist Lyric":

> Take some ordinary little event or perception, and blow it up into a quivering epiphany. Do it without adjectives if possible, or any overt use of rhetoric. Employ only the first person singular, and the Plain Style. Make what you are saying sound somehow important or serious or urgent, even if it is as opaque as a tar pit.

A perfect example of this recipe is William Carlos Williams's poem about the plums:

This Is Just to Say

I have eaten
the plums

that were in
the icebox

and which
you were probably
saving
for breakfast.

Forgive me
they were delicious
so sweet
and so cold

Another is Ezra Pound's "In a Station of the Metro":

The apparition of these faces in the crowd:
Petals, on a wet, black bough.

Both of these poems are attempts to incarnate the modernist aims of *immediacy* and *indirection*, the first by describing an utterly mundane event and pumping it up with the helium of pseudoreference; the second by taking a visual impression and wrenching it into a suppressed metaphor. Are they good poems? Well, yes, I suppose so—if you like that sort of thing. It's a matter of personal taste. To me they are crabbed, pinched, and minimalist, and represent what the poet Henry Weinfield once described to me as "American Puritanism applied to poetic expression." Such poems are like haiku—reading more than three of them at a sitting is mentally enervating.

There's something else to be noted. A fellow poet once wrote to me saying "How can anyone take the dictates of modernism seriously, when Pound and Eliot obviously didn't?" And he's right. Take a look at Pound's poem: there's the abstract noun *apparition*, and the paired adjectives *wet* and *black*. Williams's poem uses three: *delicious*, *sweet*, and *cold*. Besides this, you can run through Pound's oeuvre and find dozens of quaint uses of *thee* and *thou*, and *hast* and *hath*. As for abstractions, how about Eliot's "Superfetation of *to en*"? Or Wallace Stevens's "Complacencies of the peignoir"? As for over-the-top archaic adjective-mongering, can anyone beat the Imagist Amy Lowell's "Firesouled, vermilion-hearted"?

It seems a safe conclusion that the early modernist theorists thought up a lot of regulations that modernist poets simply ignored. But they're still being imposed on the rest of us by the MFA martinets who run poetry workshops.

In any case, let's now talk about the errors that the Poetry Establishment doesn't want to discuss, for prejudicial reasons of its own. These ones haven't been trumpeted like the five above-mentioned errors. But they can be just as deadly, and they are a lot more common. Here goes:

1. *Writing in a tone of Portentous Hush.* I discussed this error at length in my essay "Why Poetry Is Dying" at the Expansive Poetry On-Line website some years back. No one—not even the redoubtable Philip Hobsbaum—dared to address my argument on this point.

2. *Worrying about audience response.* This is like worrying about a tectonic plate shift. It's utterly futile. Your only concern should be your poem. That's what you can control.

3. *Keeping the register of one's diction strictly colloquial.* The English language is a magnificent treasure bequeathed to us by centuries of literary achievement. And you're going to write all your poems using the Fourth-Grade Basal Vocabulary List? Grow up.

4. *Composing poems based solely on one's personal experiences.* Unless you've had a life comparable to Casanova's, that's going to be pretty boring, don't you think? Poetry is fictive—the very word *poeisis* in Greek means "making things up." The medieval Scots called poets "makars" (makers) for this reason. If you can't lie, you can't be a poet.

5. *Believing that there are "No ideas but in things."* This is like believing that there is "No wine but in barrels," or "No whores but in brothels." It's just a silly slogan invented by a pediatrician in New Jersey. Ideas are everywhere, including books, your mind, daily conversation, and the Platonic realm beyond the cave, just to name a few places.

In the case of these five errors, mainstream poetry circles are unwilling even to admit that they are pitfalls. Why? It's just not good for business.

Absolutely no one will say a word about the Portentous Hush problem. Audience response? Everyone, from laureate to State Poetry Society poetaster, is desperately anxious to cultivate it. Keeping diction simple and colloquial is practically a religion in the chatrooms and workshops. Shoals of worthless poets write because they think you want to hear about their "personal experiences." As for the cliché No ideas but in things, well… it's one of those grotesque lies to which everyone is forced to pay public lip service, like "All men are created equal," or "Democracy rests upon the consent of the governed." Asking the Poetry Establishment to point out and condemn these very profitable errors would be like asking Wall Street to speak out against easy credit. It ain't gonna happen.

And to be perfectly fair, these five errors (just like the earlier five) are subject to exception whenever a poet feels that he is aesthetically required to commit one of them. As I mentioned, all strictures against poetic pitfalls are in the nature of rules for behavior in a playground. We tell children to wait their turn to shoot hoops, and to not take sand out of the sandbox, and not to pull Samantha's pigtails. All these are useful guidelines, but they aren't the basis for a full-blown system of morality. In the same way, the strictures against the ten poetic pitfalls aren't the basis for a full-blown system of aesthetics. Like everything else in the arts, they are just rules of thumb.

Be aware of all ten pitfalls, and don't skew your attention solely to those ones that the modernists warn you about. Are you going to avoid excessive use of adjectives? Fine—but also recognize that a relentlessly Plain-Style colloquial diction will prevent your poems from soaring. Are you going to stay away from abstract nouns? Fine—but recall that human beings have brains as well as senses. Are you planning to eschew any editorializing? Fine—but remember that if you resolutely say nothing, people will wonder why the hell you picked up a pen in the first place.

The crucial element in poetic composition is the poet's interior conviction that he is free to say what he wants without being hobbled by orthodoxy or—as is more common these days—a climate of received opinion. Whatever his degree of training, whatever his level of reading, whatever his native skill—if he lacks that interior conviction his art will be strangled in the cradle. And that is why I say to all poets the following:

If anyone tells you that poetic guidelines and rules of thumb are anything more than mere conveniences, regard that person, for all practical purposes, as an enemy.

The Apotheosis of Washington by Constantino Brumidi, 1865, fresco.

A Review of *Legends of Liberty Volume 1*, T A J Classics, 2021, by Andrew Benson Brown

by James Sale

Legends of Liberty is an important new poem from the American poet Andrew Benson Brown. The nearest work that one might compare it to is probably Byron's mock-epic, *Don Juan*. It is comparable because both choose serious—heroic—subject matters, yet both contrive to make fun of and send-up their heroes (and the topics), but in doing so aspects of the seriousness remain; in other words, they provide a kind of running critique of society's mores and values. In the case of Benson Brown we are covering the alleged events that constitute the American War for Independence.

Second, they both embrace narrative as a primary feature of their work: this is all about stories, not lyrics. This means there is an ongoing drive in the verse and a deep anticipation of "what next?" as the verse unfolds: we want to read on to find out more. Lyrics are perfect for depicting brief and intense emotional states, or intellectual conundrums, whereas narrative holds our attention for a much more prolonged period and provides an opportunity for a much wider sweep of an issue.

Third, they both employ ingeniously tight and classical forms. In the case of Byron this is ottava rima, a notoriously difficult Italian form that rhymes abababcc, which means alternate triple rhymes for the first six lines, and final rhyming couplet to deliver the punchline. Triples rhymes are very difficult in English compared with Italian, whose words have more natural rhymes available; Benson Brown has created a ten-line stanzaic form that rhymes ababcdcdee. This avoids the problem of triple rhymes—a good move—but adds substantial space in which to develop his materials, whilst at the same time keeping the couplet punchline at the end of the stanza; and on the subject of extra space, the final line is extended to be an alexandrine, whereas the rest are pentameters.

With this background, then, how has Benson Brown performed in writing this mock epic? Surprisingly, since this seems his first attempt at a long narrative poem, superbly well. There are many gems in this poem which need to be viewed, and—to mix metaphors—need to be savored!

One of the key tests for me of outstanding poetry—possibly of great poetry—is what I call "the quotability quotient." I notice that the great poets of the past—and clearly Shakespeare preeminently—are always being quoted: it's one line, sometimes two, but somehow we call their words to mind when reality confronts us and they seem to have encapsulated it somehow in anticipation of our predicament! Before giving an example, let me just note that this is the opposite of today's modernist and post-modernist poets: who quotes them? Except when they are being reviewed by their friends in so-called "quality" journals, nobody. Whereas, Robert Frost, for example, we quote all the time—"good fences make good neighbors," "and that has made all the difference," and "miles to go before I sleep," and so on.

Another way of putting this is that really good or great poetry often has an aphoristic quality, and this tendency was itself expressed by a great poet, Alexander Pope, some 300 years or so ago: "What oft was thought but ne'er so well expressed." Exactly—great poets write about reality, not about the solipsistic drivel of their egos. Let me, therefore, show you three wonderful aphorisms from Benson Brown's poem:

> False surfaces, once magnified, see larger truths.
> (Chapter 1: Invocation)

Beneath the "surfaces of things," even false things, there are truths we can apprehend; this is very succinctly and powerfully put.

> Said Dante: "Men don't sing in Hell, they scream.
> No melodies are found in endless death."
> (Chapter 2: Thomas Jefferson in Hell)

I have quoted the preceding line here, to indicate the authority of Dante speaking, but what a stunning, concise expression: "no melodies …"

> They're diplomats by trade—we call them hypocrites.
> (Chapter 2: Thomas Jefferson in Hell)

Finally—for there are dozens more of these aphoristic lines—something in the modern world we are all too familiar with: the diplomat and their almost unbreakable association with hypocrisy. The satire here is almost independent of its context—we know this to be true. And before leaving Benson Brown's aphoristic power, it needs be said that this fact arises because his poetry is about something, it means something. That is so refreshing in these post-modern times.

A second test for great poetry is the technical test: this relates to syntax, meter, sound effects, and so on. How deftly are these handled? Clearly, this is too much to cover in this short overview, but I think of all these technical issues the most important for a mock-epic à la Byron is the rhyming; for *Don Juan* is so funny precisely because of its rhyming prowess. In Canto XI stanza 55 he writes:

> Even I—albeit I'm sure I did not know it,
> Nor sought of foolscap subjects to be king,—
> Was reckon'd, a considerable time,
> The grand Napoleon of the realms of rhyme.

Byron is the "grand Napoleon of rhyme." Can Benson Brown match any of this? Yes, he can. The poem is wonderfully inventive and very funny because of the fecundity of rhyming that he deploys. Four examples will suffice:

> Where honor, valor, loyalty are slandered,
> Utopias are raised without a building standard.
> 				(Chapter 1: Invocation)

> Why there's Voltaire, Rousseau, and Diderot.
> And here, I think, is someone that you know."
> 				(Chapter 2: Thomas Jefferson in Hell)

> —"Why yes, it is her favorite jiggumbob.
> But now the hour is late—you're needed for a job."
> 				(Chapter 3: The New-World Mercury)

> Spit deadly cud. Smith's ego bade resist 'em:
> These soldiers warred with an entire ecosystem.
> 				(Chapter 5: The Old Man of Menotomy)

One need hardly comment on any of these examples are they are self-evidently funny and strained as many of Byron's were; inventive too: for example, in stanza 22 of Canto I (*Don Juan*) the narrator pokes fun at over-bearing women. The stanza concludes: "Oh ye lords of ladies intellectual, / Inform us truly, have they not hen-peck'd you all?" A strained rhyme or what? And note, too, that some of Benson Brown's lines here also have that same aphoristic quality—"Utopias are raised without a building standard"—we commented on before.

Finally, we come to a third quality that we require of great poetry. As G.K. Chesterton expressed it: "What alone can make a literary man in the ultimate sense great … is ideas; the power of generating and making vivid an incessant output of ideas." Benson Brown is full of ideas; indeed the poem is a cornucopia of them, and they start in lines one and two!

> Who sings of arms these days? Or even men?
> The seed of Adam's tucked inside Eve's apple,
> Not taking root—he showed his defect when
> Atonement trailed equality's long grapple.

Well, there's four lines at least: ostensibly we are writing about the American War for Independence, but immediately we sense the contemporary thrust of the satire: "these days" and of a manhood no longer considered heroic or capable of heroism; they are considered more like oppressors and tyrants in fact. And notice that genius second line: "The seed of Adam's tucked inside Eve's apple,"—the reversal of Adam's apple in Eve's apple, but not the physiological aspect, but the reference to the whole Fall of man—mankind—but given line 1 seemingly restricted to men only, which is amplified in lines 3 and 4 and the defect he (man) is still trying to atone for as he fails to embrace "equality." It is a brilliant and actually complex piece of writing, but seemingly simple and jocular.

Or take the final stanza from the Introduction, which in true mock epic mode invokes the Muses, or his case "Parnassus' power" plus eight specific muses (so totaling the nine!):

> Lend me Parnassus' power so I might
> Ascend its lower foothills from the grave:
> From Homer, dogs' and birds' raw appetite;
> From Virgil, founding sagas people crave;
> From Byron give polysyllabic wit;
> From Milton, light; from Dante, Hell's best features;
> From Wordsworth's wardrobe, lyric fabric knit
> With vines and buds frayed by romantic natures;
> From Ovid, fluid forms (minus the flings);
> And from the soaring swan of sweet Avon—his wings.

How witty and full of insight the listing is: due credit to Byron's "polysyllabic wit," which we have already commented on. And a nice distinction between what the epic of Milton offers him—"light"—with what Dante can provide "Hell's best features." Nice. But my favorite line is the last: calling on Shakespeare for inspiration, "his wings." Here the caesura is important—the first time in the stanza the pause occurs just before the final foot, and it's as he is saving the very best till the very last moment, for without those "wings" the verse is dead.

If I had one criticism to make of this collection, it would possibly be a carping one, and that is what occurs in Chapter 4, "The Shot Heard Round the Universe." Here I think the poet tries to be too ingenious technically, though I would be interested in other readers' perceptions. Essentially, Benson Brown attempts to mimetically replicate the confusion and anarchy of the battle scene via linguistic sound effects: to wit, and for example, in an intermittent sort of way he drops the rhyme of the final rhyming couplet, so that we have an ending like:

> And screamed—Apollo had lost all his nerve.
> In modern warfare, even gods surrender zen.

The lack of the rhyme here and in a few other places in this section I feel is a blemish rather than an enhancement. That last line I feel would be much wittier if written as:

> And screamed—Apollo had lost all his nerve.
> In modern warfare, even gods lose all their verve.

Mock-epic (unlike modern epics like, say, T.S. Eliot's *Wasteland*) requires the closure of rhyme and we feel the want of it.

But that said, one extra benefit of this collection is the extensive set of Notes at the end of it; and these are much funnier and more useful than Eliot's own for his *Wasteland*. Find out all sorts of obscure and recondite facts and information, such as who Albertinus Mussatus was! Highly readable and a wonderful complement to the poetry.

I could go on, but I think I have said enough now. Andrew Benson Brown's *Legends of Liberty* is a modern classic that should be read by all adults and taught in colleges and schools. My final criticism is that I am not sure whether this work is complete or not! As with Byron's *Don Juan* (and he did not live to complete his poem), it seems complete (as does the *Aeneid* in another way). So here—I can see it's entirely possible that Benson Brown may well extend this further—or not. But it would be good to know. I wish this collection massive success with the public in future, for it is a poem for the public—not the academics, the postmodernists and the know-it-alls, but the reading public who wish to be entertained first and foremost, and whilst that process is going on, to be educated too.

Whitman's Curse: Contemporary Poetry as Solipsism

by Adam Sedia

Contemporary poetry is plagued by several characteristic vices: obscurity, banality, nihilism—each a topic for examination in its own right. But its most glaring and even characteristic vice is an omnipresent solipsism—a narcissistic navel-gazing by which the poet elevates superficial autobiographical detail to the level of a poetic subject, with no greater end in mind than presenting his perspective either as an individual or as a member of an identity group based on race, class, or some other demographic detail.

Why is this a problem? After all, is *all* poetry not in some sense autobiographical? After all a poet can only draw material for a poem from his own experience, either lived or learned. Yes: poetry is the supreme individual expression—thought frozen in eternity through the medium of art, either oral memory or writing. But that precise nature of poetry dictates that it must be universal if it is to have any success as a poem. The poem, by definition, is the poet placing his own internal thoughts and experiences *outside* his own frame of reference, so that it directly engages the reader's own knowledge and experience.

The poet achieves this through the use of poetic metaphor—not metaphor as a simple rhetorical comparison, but metaphor in its literal sense: a "transfer" of the object to its representation. The sense-object that is poetic subject becomes poetic only through its transformation into a representation of an eternal, unchangeable, universal ideal, which because of its eternity, immutability, and universality is readily known and relatable to any reader across time and language.

"Solipsism" as defined here, declines to take the poetic leap from the temporal to the eternal, most likely because recognition of anything eternal and universal dwarfs the self—and intolerable feeling for any narcissist. This is not to say that contemporary poets are clinical narcissists. But contemporary poets, at least in the West, all grew up in a world of consumer culture and mass advertising that cater to individual self-worth and self-perception to push a product. The undeniable effect of this has been a narcissistic society—or at least a society with a narcissistic perspective.

In a sense, we cannot blame contemporary poets for being products of the societies in which they grew to adulthood. But it is the duty of the poet to break these bounds of time and custom, rising above them, as Dante rose above the world of feudal lords and warring Guelphs and Ghibellines, and Goethe above the world of hereditary aristocracy and Napoleonic world-conquest. So it is the contemporary poet's duty to rise above our world of corporate tyranny, political and marketing propaganda, and would-be world overlords to reveal truth through the lens of our time. Except contemporary poets fail in this regard. It is much more comforting to talk about oneself than speak against the powers that bestow fame and fortune.

This essay explores solipsism in contemporary American poetry, traces its history to Walt Whitman, and poses a solution and a way forward to revive poetry as true artistic representation rather than self-absorbed preening.

I

First it is useful to show exactly how this solipsism manifests itself. Contemporary American poetry is so rife with solipsism that selecting representative examples proves a difficult task. Two poets immediately come to mind, but before presenting examples from them, the world was treated very recently to a very public display of solipsistic contemporary poetry.

This egregious and very fresh example is no less than "The Hill We Climb" by Amanda Gorman, recited by her at the most recent United States presidential inauguration. The poem embodies all of the vices of contemporary poetry, from prosaic language, grammar and syntax errors, and frequent use of cliché to an awkward unevenness of its lines and an utter lack of any musicality. But beyond poetics, the poem stands as a monument to solipsism. Only eight lines in, the poem features this whopper of a line:

> We, the successors of a country and a time where a skinny Black girl descended from slaves and raised by a single mother can dream of becoming president, only to find herself reciting for one.

She has barely begun her piece, and Gorman places *herself* at the center of a poem that is ostensibly to celebrate a new government over a nation of 325 million people. It is also a shocking display of ingratitude: she wants to *be* president, not just recite for one. Nor is it even logically coherent: if she is describing her own time, how is she its successor? By inserting herself at the center of the poem like this, Gorman abdicates her central role as poet of crafting the poetic voice. A poem's narrative voice is at once personal and universal. If the ideas a poem conveys are to have any meaning to a different mind reading it, the poem must engage the reader in the experience described beyond the level of mere amusement or sensory titillation. The poet's experience must *mean something* to the reader. To achieve this effect, upon which the entire success of a poem depends, the poet must step outside his own frame of reference and view it as the reader would.

Gorman does not do this. Instead, she describes herself in raw demographic terms and relates her experience standing there, reciting at the inauguration. She makes no attempt at insight beyond a cliché "anyone can dream of becoming president" motivational slogan. By adopting such a myopic perspective, Gorman destroys any chance the poem has of appealing to a universal audience—one reflective of the whole nation. Instead, she speaks on behalf of Amanda Gorman and no one else.

But Gorman is not the only navel-gazing poet to have recited at a presidential inauguration. Richard Blanco, who recited at Barack Obama's second inauguration in 2013, like Gorman, also wears his identity on his sleeve—in his case as a homosexual and the son of Cuban immigrants. A particularly glaring example of solipsism from his poetry includes the following lines from his 2012 poem, "Looking for the Gulf Motel." The poem begins very autobiographically:

There should be nothing here I don't remember...

> The Gulf Motel with mermaid lampposts
> and ship's wheel in the lobby should still be
> rising out of the sand like a cake decoration.
> My brother and I should still be pretending
> we don't know our parents, embarrassing us
> as they roll the luggage cart past the front desk
> loaded with our scruffy suitcases, two-dozen
> loaves of Cuban bread, brown bags bulging
> with enough mangos to last the entire week,
> our espresso pot, the pressure cooker- and
> a pork roast reeking garlic through the lobby.
> All because we can't afford to eat out, not even
> on vacation, only two hours from our home
> in Miami, but far enough away to be thrilled
> by whiter sands on the west coast of Florida,
> where I should still be for the first time watching
> the sun set instead of rise over the ocean.

It then continues, repeating the italicized refrain, "There should be nothing here I don't remember . . . ," three more times, each followed by intimate, photographic details from Blanco's childhood, with particular focus on scenes unique to his parents' Cuban immigrant background.

At best, Blanco only hints at a universal theme in the poem: the desire to hold onto memories from childhood. But he never hints at why these memories are important to him. Yes, they define his experience in his formative years—experience that no doubt he would say formed the person he would become. He stops at wishing not to forget those memories. He declines to transform them into something to which any reader can relate. Instead, the reader is left with a "day in the life of" spectator experience, left to say, "That's nice," or "That's interesting," as an outsider, without an idea engaging him directly in the sensory experience.

"Looking for the Gulf Motel" is hardly an aberration. Blanco's poetry is rife with similar examples, much of it focusing on details relating to his identity as a Cuban-American and as a homosexual. While he is very apt at description and detail, his poetry is less a work of metaphor than of autobiography, presenting a perspective rather than an idea.

Lawrence Joseph is another poet whose work is rife with solipsistic detail. Like Blanco he is the son of immigrants—Lebanese rather than

Cuban. Uniquely, Joseph is a well-known Big Law attorney who, famously represented Texas in its suit before the United States Supreme Court challenging the 2020 election.[1]

His provocatively-titled poem "Sand Nigger," published in his 1988 volume *Curriculum Vitae*, captures the solipsism rife in his poetry:

> . . .
> Lebanon of mountains and sea,
> of pine and almond trees,
> of cedars in the service
> of Solomon, Lebanon
> of Babylonians, Phoenicians, Arabs, Turks
> and Byzantines, of the one-eyed
> monk, saint Maron,
> in whose rite I am baptized;
> Lebanon of my mother
> warning my father not to let
> the children hear,
> of my brother who hears
> and from whose silence
> I know there is something
> I will never know; Lebanon
> of grandpa giving me my first coin
> secretly, secretly
> holding my face in his hands,
> kissing me and promising me
> the whole world.
> My father's vocal chords bleed;
> he shouts too much
> at his brother, his partner,
> in the grocery store that fails.
> I hide money in my drawer, I have
> the talent to make myself heard.
> I am admonished to learn,
> never to dirty my hands
> with sawdust and meat.
> . . .
> "Sand nigger," I'm called,
> and the name fits: I am
> the light-skinned nigger

> with black eyes and the look
> difficult to figure – a look
> of indifference, a look to kill –
> a Levantine nigger
> in the city on the strait
> between the great lakes Erie and St. Clair
> which has a reputation
> for violence, an enthusiastically
> bad-tempered sand nigger
> who waves his hands, nice enough
> to pass, Lebanese enough
> to be against his brother,
> with his brother against his cousin,
> with cousin and brother
> against the stranger.

Joseph is obviously not writing strictly about himself. The last few lines of the poem generalize his experience enough to make it clear that he is writing of the Lebanese and the Arab immigrant experience more generally, with a rather harsh view of what he sees as fractious behavior endemic to that community.

Still, he goes no further than that. He portrays the experience of a community, which while it might present a new perspective to the reader, does not engage the reader directly. It falls short of transferring the generalized Lebanese and Arab immigrant experience into the realm of the universal, even though the subject might easily lend itself to a discussion of displacement or perceptions of time and place more generally. Joseph does not go there.

Like Blanco, he presents his own and his family's experience as a "day in the life of" portrayal, with little beyond that except a reflection on negative traits among the Lebanese. The episodes he describes of the interactions between his family members, while they might offer glimpses at unique scenes and individuals, are little more than anecdotes. No metaphor transfers them into anything greater than exemplars of what Joseph sees as defects in the Lebanese character.

Also like Blanco, Joseph places his identity at the center of his description: Lebanese, Catholic, the son of immigrants. Touting these identities so openly is but a manifestation of solipsism. Cultural, ethnic, and religious background is one—albeit a superficial—way to define the self as an entity distinct from others. But while Joseph—and Blanco—

showcase their identities, they never directly engage the reader with it. Instead, it languishes in the realm of mere description—a mere anthropological study written in the first person

Gorman, Blanco, and Joseph are very much mainstream, establishment poets. Their work reflects what the dominant cultural and educational institutions hold out as good poetry. Solipsism, it would seem, is the dominant trend in contemporary poetry. To understand why poetry is there, it helps to understand how it arrived there.

II

Autobiographical poems, of course, are nothing new. Poets did not start writing poems about themselves until a generation ago. Indeed, no less a master than John Milton produced an autobiographical poem that stands as one of the most famous works in the English language, the sonnet "On His Blindness":

> When I consider how my light is spent
> Ere half my days, in this dark world and wide;
> And that one talent which is death to hide,
> Lodged with me useless, though my soul more bent
> To serve therewith my Maker, and present
> My true account, lest he returning chide:
> Doth God exact day-labor, light denied,
> I fondly ask? But Patience, to prevent
> That murmur, soon replies, God doth not need
> Either man's work or his own gifts; who best
> Bear his mild yoke, they serve him best: his state
> Is kingly; thousands at his bidding speed,
> And post o'er land and ocean without rest;
> They also serve who only stand and wait.

Here, Milton discusses not only his being stricken with blindness but also the thoughts it provokes within him. It is personal in the sense that Milton describes his own perspective on his own experience. Yet Milton does not revel in his status as the sufferer of a disability. He does not ask the reader to empathize with him as a blind man—as both Blanco and Joseph do as the sons of immigrants. Instead, he asks how his affliction is part of the Divine Will for him, and in wrestling with that question

Illustration from *The Poetical Works of John Milton*. Original held and digitized by the British Library.

famously resolves the issue: serving God—or fulfilling one's role more generally—may be achieved passively as much as actively.

Milton universalizes his experience. He uses his blindness as an object to achieve poetic metaphor, and in so doing uses it as a vehicle to reveal a greater truth. The sonnet is not so much about Milton himself as the realization he achieves in considering an experience. The only thing autobiographical is that Milton considers his own state, rather than an external object.

A century and a half later, the Romantic poets, with their emphasis on poetry as the product of emotion, placed special emphasis on the deeply personal nature of poetry. Wordsworth, in famously defining poetry as "the spontaneous overflow of powerful feelings . . . from emotion recollected in tranquility,"[2] captured the Romantic view of poetry as the product of emotion—a deeply individual experience inexorably intertwined with the poet's unique sensory experience. If poetry is simply recollected emotion, the poet's primary duty is the accurate conveyance of the emotion rather than a reflection on some universal truth. Metaphor is relegated to a supporting role; the description is what counts, as it is the primary vehicle for conveying emotion.

Wordsworth's thirteen-book *The Prelude* is an oddity among epic poems: the grandiose, sweeping epic form juxtaposed against its subject matter: intimate and often mundane scenes from Wordsworth's own life. Indeed, the poem is an extended autobiography, rife with reminiscences and reflections on the events and scenes of Wordsworth's life, with particular focus on his childhood and youth.

A good example of the self-referential episodes in *The Prelude* is the portrayal of Wordsworth's wanderings in the wilderness at eight years old:

> Fair seed-time had my soul, and I grew up
> Fostered alike by beauty and by fear;
> Much favored in my birthplace, and no less
> In that beloved Vale to which, erelong,
> I was transplanted. Well I call to mind
> ('Twas at an early age, ere I had seen
> Nine summers) when upon the mountain slope
> The frost and breath of frosty wind had snapped
> The last autumnal crocus, 'twas my joy
> To wander half the night among the Cliffs
> And the smooth Hollows, where the woodcocks ran

> Along the open turf. In thought and wish
> That time, my shoulder all with springes hung,
> I was a fell destroyer. On the heights
> Scudding away from snare to snare, I plied
> My anxious visitation, hurrying on,
> Still hurrying, hurrying onward; moon and stars
> Were shining o'er my head; I was alone,
> And seemed to be a trouble to the peace
> That was among them. . . .
>
> *(The Prelude,* I:305-24.)

Here Wordsworth sounds almost contemporary, sharing details of his boyhood that, while vividly descriptive, seem more oriented towards Wordsworth expounding his life's story than universalizing the experience through metaphor. Indeed, few readers, particularly contemporary readers, can relate directly to Wordsworth's experience as an eight-year-old boy alone in the wilderness. If anything, it seems most notable as a historical curiosity.

But Wordsworth does more than string together mere autobiographical sketches. After all this description he waxes truly poetic:

> The mind of Man is framed even like the breath
> And harmony of music. There is a dark
> Invisible workmanship that reconciles
> Discordant elements, and makes them move
> In one society. Ah me! That all
> The terrors, all the early miseries,
> Regrets, vexations, lassitudes, that all
> The thoughts and feelings which have been infused
> Into my mind, should ever have made up
> The calm existence that is mine when I
> Am worthy of myself! Praise to the end!
> Thanks likewise for the means!
>
> (I:351-62.)

At last Wordsworth universalizes the experience. His youthful wanderings formed the man he became and in them he sees destiny at work. And for that he is grateful. It is not a particularly novel or insightful observation, but one Wordsworth clearly makes in earnest.

The Prelude follows this general pattern throughout: a description of an quotidian experience from Wordsworth's early life along with the emotions he experienced at the time followed by a reflection on the deeper, universalized significance of the experience. The poem in this way might be called a "didactic autobiography."

Didactic as it may be, Wordsworth's explications in *The Prelude* fall short of true poetic metaphor. Wordsworth tells his intent and meaning outright, rather than revealing the meaning through transformation of the poetic object. Though he "tells" rather than "shows," Wordsworth nonetheless universalizes his experiences and provides a meaning for them presented as a lesson to the reader.

The Prelude represents a departure from the traditional epic. The very mundaneness of its episodes and the intimacy of its description turns the genre on its head. But more importantly, it represents a shift away from autobiographical poetry in the style of Milton. In making himself the subject of an entire thirteen-book epic, Wordsworth showed the way for poetry to devolve into navel-gazing. As close as it comes, *The Prelude* does not achieve that feat on its own; it still presents autobiographical details as instructive of a greater lesson. Wordsworth still feels that he must provide something to the reader in the form of a lesson when he relates his life experiences. He did not yet take the leap of making autobiography both the subject and the end of his poetry.

III

The Prelude was only a prelude. Across the Atlantic, the romantic trends in poetry would blossom into true solipsism in the works of Walt Whitman.

Whitman's impact on American poetry was nothing short of transformational. Before him, American poets like Edgar Allan Poe and William Cullen Bryant wrote in the classical style inherited from Europe. Whitman gave the still-young nation a new style: discursive, conversational, non-formal, and deeply intimate. Whitman more than anyone paved the way for contemporary free verse. Indeed, Ezra Pound acknowledged as much in his poem "A Pact":

> I make a pact with you, Walt Whitman –
> I have detested you long enough.
> I come to you as a grown child

> Who has had a pig-headed father;
> I am old enough now to make friends.
> It was you that broke the new wood,
> Now is a time for carving.
> We have one sap and one root –
> Let there be commerce between us.

For Pound to proclaim that he and Whitman shared "one sap and one root" and to compare himself to a "grown child" returning to Whitman as his father is as clear an acknowledgment of influence as a poet can make. As profoundly influential as Pound was on the modernist movement in poetry, his statement renders Whitman no less than the forefather of modernism in poetry.

But Whitman is the forefather of more than the modernist style and aesthetic. Whitman is truly the first and perhaps the greatest solipsistic poet. One of Whitman's most famous works is the masterpiece of solipsism, the sprawling, 1,346-line "Song of Myself."

The poem begins with a clear statement of intent:

> I celebrate myself, and sing myself,
> And what I assume you shall assume,
> For every atom belonging to me as good belongs to you.
> I loafe and invite my soul,
> I lean and loafe at my ease observing a spear of summer grass.
> My tongue, every atom of my blood, form'd from this soil, this air,
> Born here of parents born here from parents the same, and their parents the same,
> I, now thirty-seven years old in perfect health begin,
> Hoping to cease not till death.
> Creeds and schools in abeyance,
> Retiring back a while sufficed at what they are, but never forgotten,
> I harbor for good or bad, I permit to speak at every hazard,
> Nature without check with original energy.
>
> (ll. 1-13.)

Whitman could not be clearer. Not for him is Wordsworth's didactic use of autobiography. Rather, he seeks only to "celebrate myself." The declaration to the reader "every atom belonging to me as good belongs to you" is not a statement of shared humanity as much as an invitation to step inside Whitman's own frame of reference and see the world as he sees it. And he says later:

> You shall no longer take things at second or third hand, nor look through the eyes of the dead, nor feed on the spectres in books,
> You shall not look through my eyes either, nor take things from me,
> You shall listen to all sides and filter them from your self.
> (ll. 35-37.)

Whitman is a democratic solipsist. He wants the reader to celebrate the self as much as he does, to view the world through a self-referential frame as much as he does. What would otherwise be an insufferable narcissism becomes an enticement: the poem does not ask the reader to endure Whitman's navel-gazing but to join him in it, to see his own experiences reflected in the mirror of those Whitman describes from his own life.

The bulk of the poem, consequently, is an exposition of autobiographical minutiae rendered in vivid descriptive detail. Whitman bombards the reader with the scenes he saw traveling across America in the 1850s, descriptions of people, places, and events—portrayals of everyday life filtered through his own lens of observation.

The intimacy of Whitman's detail also takes an additional dimension. Whitman, much ahead of his time, gives frank descriptions of sexual experiences throughout the poem, enough to cause Boston's district attorney to write to Whitman's publisher threatening prosecution under Massachusetts's obscenity laws.[3]

Interspersed throughout the scenic portrayals, Whitman inserts his own thoughts and insights. Unlike Wordsworth, these are not didactic, but self-reflective. Some, indeed, go far beyond self-reflection and verge on the megalomaniacal. In the following two passages, Whitman proclaims a sort of divinity for himself:

> Divine am I inside and out, and I make holy whatever I touch or am touch'd from,
> The scent of these arm-pits aroma finer than prayer,
> This head more than churches, bibles, and all the creeds.

> If I worship one thing more than another it shall be the spread of my own body, or any part of it,
> . . .
>
> (ll. 524-27.)

> Why should I pray? why should I venerate and be ceremonious?
> Having pried through the strata, analyzed to a hair, counsel'd with doctors and calculated close,
> I find no sweeter fat than sticks to my own bones.
> In all people I see myself, none more and not one a barley-corn less,
> And the good or bad I say of myself I say of them.
> I know I am solid and sound,
> To me the converging objects of the universe perpetually flow,
> All are written to me, and I must get what the writing means.
> I know I am deathless,
> I know this orbit of mine cannot be swept by a carpenter's compass,
> I know I shall not pass like a child's carlacue cut with a burnt stick at night.
> I know I am august,
> I do not trouble my spirit to vindicate itself or be understood,
> I see that the elementary laws never apologize,
> (I reckon I behave no prouder than the level I plant my house by, after all.)
> I exist as I am, that is enough,
> If no other in the world be aware I sit content,
> And if each and all be aware I sit content.
> One world is aware and by far the largest to me, and that is myself,
> And whether I come to my own to-day or in ten thousand or ten million years,
> I can cheerfully take it now, or with equal cheerfulness I can wait.
>
> (ll. 398-418.)

In a no less grandiose flourish, he offers his self-analysis of his own role as poet:

> I am the poet of the Body and I am the poet of the Soul,
> The pleasures of heaven are with me and the pains of hell are with me,
> The first I graft and increase upon myself, the latter I translate into a new tongue.
> I am the poet of the woman the same as the man,
> And I say it is as great to be a woman as to be a man,
> And I say there is nothing greater than the mother of men.
> I chant the chant of dilation or pride,
> We have had ducking and deprecating about enough,
> I show that size is only development.
> Have you outstript the rest? are you the President?
> It is a trifle, they will more than arrive there every one, and still pass on.
> I am he that walks with the tender and growing night,
> I call to the earth and sea half-held by the night.
>
> (ll. 422-34.)

Or, more famously:

> Do I contradict myself?
> Very well then I contradict myself,
> (I am large, I contain multitudes.)
>
> (ll. 1324-26.)

And perhaps most solipsistic of all, Whitman proclaims that he is the pinnacle of all creation up to then:

> I am an acme of things accomplish'd, and I an encloser of things to be.
> My feet strike an apex of the apices of the stairs,
> On every step bunches of ages, and larger bunches between the steps,
> All below duly travel'd, and still I mount and mount.
> Rise after rise bow the phantoms behind me,
> Afar down I see the huge first Nothing, I know I was even there,
> I waited unseen and always, and slept through the lethargic mist,
> And took my time, and took no hurt from the fetid carbon.

> Long I was hugg'd close—long and long.
> Immense have been the preparations for me,
> Faithful and friendly the arms that have helped me.
> Cycles ferried my cradle, rowing and rowing like cheerful boatmen,
> For room to me stars kept aside in their own rings,
> They sent influences to look after what was to hold me.
> Before I was born out of my mother generations guided me,
> My embryo has never been torpid, nothing could overlay it.
> For it the nebula cohered to an orb,
> The long slow strata piled to rest it on,
> Vast vegetables gave it sustenance,
> Monstrous sauroids transported it in their mouths and deposited it with care.
> All forces have been steadily employed to complete and delight me,
>
> Now on this spot I stand with my robust soul.
> (ll. 1148-69.)

The stars, the dinosaurs, human history—all were but one great preface, preparing the universe for the appearance of Walt Whitman.

But Whitman does not make these assertions from a tone of superiority. Indeed, considered in the context of the rest of the poem, with its intimate detail of everyday experiences, the reader is left with the impression that what Whitman proclaims about himself holds true just as much for anyone else. It is that equal-opportunity solipsism, that invitation to share in self-celebration and self-admiration that makes Whitman enticing rather than insufferable.

At the end of the poem, Whitman ponders his mortality and what will become of him after death:

> The last scud of day holds back for me,
> It flings my likeness after the rest and true as any on the shadowed wilds,
> It coaxes me to the vapor and the dusk.
> I depart as air, I shake my white locks at the runaway sun,
> I effuse my flesh in eddies, and drift it in lacy jags.
> I bequeath myself to the dirt to grow from the grass I love,
> If you want me again look for me under your boot-soles.

> You will hardly know who I am or what I mean,
> But I shall be good health to you nevertheless,
> And filter and fibre your blood.
> Failing to fetch me at first keep encouraged,
> Missing me one place search another,
> I stop somewhere waiting for you.
>
> (ll. 1334-46.)

He is clearly not a believer in the immortality of the soul. In a twist of irony, Whitman, the living divinity for whom all of geologic time was a mere preparation, "bequeath[s]" himself "to the dirt," to be found only "under your boot-soles." For Whitman, divinity is found in living, and the divine existence ceases on death.

Yet Whitman's self survives and remains the focus of the poem, even after death. In its final line, "I stop somewhere waiting for you," Whitman remains as an idea, if not an entity, waiting for discovery by the reader, to be "good health" to him. Even after what he sees as his own annihilation, Whitman never removes himself as the center and focus of the poem.

"Song of Myself" is the supreme manifesto of solipsism. It offers no didactic lesson and examines no universal truth beyond celebrating the self as the center and pinnacle of all existence. How Whitman sees his own self is how he would have everyone see their own selves: the only true frame of reference, free from and above all creeds, philosophies, and societal and cultural mores.

And Whitman triumphed. By and large, society, especially in America, has adopted his view of the self as the supreme arbiter of truth, the only frame of reference by which to judge the external world. Even among those professing a religion or adhering to a philosophy, they justify their belief or acceptance in terms of the self, their own experiences, and their own frame of reference. Solipsism lies at the core of contemporary American thought. Whitman was only its most effusive prophet.

It invites no wonder, then, that poets in such a solipsistic culture write solipsistic verse. They write from what they know and experience in their lives. But what, when all is written and published, does the solipsistic mindset achieve through poetry?

IV

Solipsism may be the way of the world, but much like consumer products sold by appeals to selfish desires, it can ultimately never satisfy the human longing for meaning that poetry addresses. All it can offer is cheap thrills. It is shallow; it portrays an experience in which the reader might—or might not—see a reflection of his own life, but it never transforms the individual experience into a depersonalized revelation of a universal truth. Without that transformative leap, poetry remains nothing more than autobiography, an anthropological curiosity locked within time and space, rather than a universal ideal that transcends them.

Where does that leave poetry? Is Whitman's legacy inescapable? Whitman might be the patriarch of modernism and solipsism in American poetry, but he is far from the only model for poets. Indeed, a slightly older contemporary and fellow countryman of his can show today's poets an alternative course. That poet is Henry Wadsworth Longfellow.

Famous for his epics *The Song of Hiawatha* and *Evangeline* and his Chaucer-inspired *Tales of a Wayside Inn*, Longfellow wrote scores of shorter poems among which few are in any way autobiographical. When he does wax autobiographical, however, Longfellow follows the model of Milton, universalizing his experience.

"My Lost Youth," an early poem published in his 1847 volume, *Birds of Passage*, is perhaps the best example of such a poem. In fact, it is very much in the vein of Blanco's "Looking for the Gulf Motel" or Joseph's "Sand Nigger"—a description of childhood experience viewed in hindsight by the adult poet. Unlike those poems, however, Longfellow does not merely recount the thoughts and emotions evoked upon visiting his childhood home and the places he frequented as a boy; he uses them as a vehicle to reveal a greater, universal truth.

The poem begins by describing his return to his native town in Maine:

> Often I think of the beautiful town
> That is seated by the sea;
> Often in thought go up and down
> The pleasant streets of that dear old town,
> And my youth comes back to me.
> And a verse of a Lapland song
> Is haunting my memory still:

> "A boy's will is the wind's will,
> And the thoughts of youth are long, long thoughts."

The Lappish song quoted at the end of the stanza is repeated as a refrain at the end of each of the poem's ten stanzas. Attributing these thoughts to a distant people who sang it in a strange tongue subtly emphasizes the universality of the ideas they express. The realization that the thoughts of childhood form the adult is not Longfellow's own, but a human condition that transcends any individual or society.

He describes the scenes of the town and its surrounding countryside and the thoughts and emotions they evoke. He makes perhaps his most poignant and powerful observations in the seventh and eighth stanzas:

> I remember the gleams and glooms that dart
> Across the schoolboy's brain;
> The song and the silence in the heart,
> That in part are prophecies, and in part
> Are longings wild and vain.
> . . .
> There are things of which I may not speak;
> There are dreams that cannot die;
> There are thoughts that make the strong heart weak,
> And bring a pallor into the cheek,
> And a mist before the eye.
> . . .

Here he describes an experience at once his own and at the same time not necessarily his—capable of recognition in every reader who has survived long enough to realize their youth has flown. Although he mourns his youth long gone, at the same time he recognizes that many of its fleeting experiences and thoughts have remained, and often influenced the adult that the child would one day become. Unlike Wordsworth, Longfellow does not relate this lesson directly, in didactic fashion. Instead, he describes the general effect and impression of his childhood thoughts and experiences without ever diving into the intimate detail that both Blanco and Joseph use to illustrate their experiences. This at once specific and generalized narrative universalizes the experience, leading the reader to a realization of a universal truth he recognizes, instead of an autobiography that achieves little beyond presenting a personal story.

Henry Wadsworth Longfellow Memorial, sculpture by Daniel Chester French, 1913. Photo by Daderot.

Though Longfellow addresses the same subject matter as Blanco and Joseph, and indeed as Whitman and Wordsworth, he describes and uses it in a completely different way. Both the experiences of childhood and the impressions they leave on the adult are used metaphorically, to reveal a truth about the human condition as it is affected by the passage of time. That is the only real sense in which any reader should care what a poet's childhood experiences were—by viewing through them the truths they reveal.

Autobiography certainly has a place in poetry. Indeed, autobiography is an unavoidable element of poetry. But autobiography for its own sake is not poetic, it is mere navel-gazing. Even when used to illustrate the perceived experiences of a larger community, it does nothing more than shout to the reader, "Look at me!" Autobiography instead should be used as a device to serve the poetic end: revelation of truth through metaphor. Milton and Longfellow show how to do this successfully, and true poetry will emulate them and their timeless revelations instead of the solipsism of Whitman and his heirs of the present day.

Notes

1. Domestico, Anthony. "So Many Selves: A Poet of Unlikely Combinations." *Commonweal.* Mar. 17, 2020. Available at https://www.commonwealmagazine.org/compound-voices.
2. From the Preface to *Lyrical Ballads* (1802).
3. Folsom, Ed, and Jerome Loving. Notes to "The Walt Whitman Controversy" by Mark Twain. *Virginia Quarterly Review.* Spring 2007. Available at https://www.vqronline.org/vqr-symposium/walt-whitman-controversy.

Poets

Adams, Haydn is a graduate of Durham and Cambridge Universities and retired after 40 years in education, the last twenty spent in China. Currently he lives in the United Kingdom. His publications include the novels *The Spinner of The Years, Ecstatic from One Lie,* and *Catching Mice,* all available from Amazon, and poems in university magazines and some anthologies—mostly now out of print.

Anderson, C.B. was the longtime gardener for the PBS television series *The Victory Garden.* Hundreds of his poems have appeared in scores of print and electronic journals out of North America, Great Britain, Ireland, Austria, Australia, and India. His collection *Mortal Soup and the Blue Yonder* was published in 2013 by White Violet Press and his newest collection *Roots in the Sky, Boots on the Ground* was published by Kelsay Books in 2019.

Arredondo, Anna J. is a Pennsylvania native now residing in Colorado. She is an engineer by education, a home educator by choice, and by preference, a poet.

Austin, Peter is a retired professor of English who lives in Toronto.

Benson Brown, Andrew was a graduate student at George Mason University before taking too many classes outside his discipline coincided with the reality of Debt. He now works as a children's caseworker in rural Missouri. In his spare time he reads obscure classics, writes things of little market value, and exercises far more than is befitting for a modern intellectual.

Bhattacharya, Sarban is a young poet and classicist currently pursuing a master's degree in English literature.

Bianchi, Radhika lives in Santiago, Chile (her mother's birthplace) and is an artist and English teacher. She was raised in Los Angeles, California.

Bryant, Mike is a poet and retired plumber living on the Gulf Coast of Texas. He is the Moderator for the Society of Classical Poets website.

Bryant, Susan Jarvis is the winner of the 2020 International SCP Poetry Competition and has been nominated for the 2022 Pushcart Prize.

Caylor, Duane is a physician in Dubuque, Iowa.

Canerdy, Janice is a retired high-school English teacher from Potts Camp, Mississippi. Her first book, *Expressions of Faith* (Christian Faith Publishing), was published in December 2016.

Christie, Sandi is a medical technician who lives in Florida. She has published two works *A Course in Miracles: Miracles Fall Like Drops of Rain,* and *Lilies of Forgiveness.*

Chuba, A.S. is thirteen years old and attends Maryvale Academy in Canada.

Coats, Margaret lives in California. She holds a Ph.D. in English and American literature and language from Harvard University. She has retired from a career of teaching literature, languages, and writing that included considerable work in home-schooling for her own family and others.

Cook, Sally is a former Wilbur Fellow and six-time Pushcart nominee. She is a regular contributor to *National Review,* and has appeared in various venues, including *Trinacria.* Also a painter, her present works in the style known as Magic Realism are represented in national collections such as the NSDAR Museum in Washington, D.C., and the Burchfield Penney Art Center in Buffalo, New York.

Corey, Cheryl received 1st Place for the Dylan Thomas Award and Honorable Mention for the June Kraeft Memorial Award in The World Order of Narrative and Formalist Poets contest.

D'Anselmi, Luca teaches Latin and Greek. He lives in Bryn Mawr, Pennsylvania.

Darling, Jan is a New Zealander who has worked in Auckland, Wellington, London, Barcelona, New York, and Sydney at copywriting and marketing strategy. She has spent her leisure time over sixty years writing poetry and short stories. Now retired, she lives in pastoral New South Wales.

DesBois, Jack is a singer, actor, and storyteller. He gives annual Epiphany season performances of *The Western Star,* which he wrote in 2016. He self-published a chapbook of short poems in 2018. As a singer, Jack has had the good fortune to solo in several of the great works of Baroque Oratorio, including Handel's Messiah (Bass) and Esther (Haman) and J.S. Bach's St. John Passion (Jesus). Jack lives in Topsfield, Massachusetts.

Dumer, Olga was born and educated in Moscow, Russia. Both her B.A. and M.A. degrees were in English Language and Literature and she obtained her Ph.D. in Linguistics at the Russian Academy of Sciences. Since her family moved to the USA, she has been teaching English, ESL and Linguistics in California.

Eardley, Jeff lives in the heart of England near to the Peak District National Park and is a local musician who plays guitar, mandolin, and piano steeped in the music of America.

Erlandson, Cynthia is a poet and fitness professional living in Royal Oak, Michigan.

Erlandson, Paul resides in Royal Oak Michigan, and has recently retired from an automotive engineering career with Ford Motor Company.

Freeman, Paul A. is the author of *Rumours of Ophir*, a crime novel that was taught in Zimbabwean high schools and has been translated into German. In addition to having two novels, a children's book, and an 18,000-word narrative poem (*Robin Hood and Friar Tuck: Zombie Killers!*) commercially published, Paul is the author of hundreds of published short stories, poems, and articles.

Grant, Alan lives in Glastonbury, England, where he makes a regular pilgrimage to the Tor, reads Tarot, and purchases too many books.

Greene, Joseph is a pianist, composer and poet who lives in Riverside, California. He is currently a freshman student at California Baptist University working towards a Bachelor's Degree in Music Composition.

Grein, Dusty is a poet, novelist, editor, and book producer. His written work has been published in numerous magazines and books, as well as in print and online journals. He has had poetry translated into several languages worldwide, is the co-author of a book on crafting classical poetry, and his How To articles can be found reprinted in several locations. Dusty lives, works, and plays in the Pacific Northwestern United States. There he enjoys spending his time, whenever possible, spoiling many of his twenty grandchildren before sending them back home to their parents.

Goldberg, Lee (aka Rantingsenior) is a writer who lives in Naperville, Illinois. He is retired and has worked in a variety of areas including computer programming and network administration.

Haase, Lucia has several books of poetry published. She lives in Spring Valley, Illinois.

Hartley, Peter is a retired painting restorer. He was born in Liverpool and lives in Manchester, U.K. His book, *On a Boat to Barra,* was published in 2019.

Hook, Talbot is an educator and nascent writer currently living in Des Moines, Iowa.

Hsu, Matt is a twelfth-grade student at San Francisco University High School.

Huang, Clara is an eleventh-grade student at Fei Tian Academy of the Arts in New York.

Irby, David D. is a retired law enforcement officer and a U.S. Air Force veteran, currently living in Halifax, Virginia.

Jackson, Corey Elizabeth is a retired teacher and community stage actress and singer living in Aurora, Ontario, Canada.

James, Leland is the author of four poetry collections and four children's books in verse. He has published over three hundred poems in poetry venues worldwide. He was the winner of the U.K.'s *Aesthetica* Creative Writing Award and has won or received honors in many other competitions, both in the United States and Europe.

Jennings, Alison is a Seattle-based poet who taught in public schools before returning to poetry. She has also worked as editor, journalist, and accountant. Visit her website at sites.google.com/view/airandfirepoet/home.

Kalouria, Tonia, a former Spanish teacher and "soap" actress, is now a poet in Chagrin Falls, Ohio.

Kemper, Daniel is a systems engineer living in California.

Kemper, Jeff has been a biology teacher, biblical studies instructor, editor, and painting contractor. He lives in York County, Pennsylvania.

Kinsky, Carl is a country lawyer living in Ste. Genevieve, Missouri.

Koren, Judy, from Haifa, Israel, has a degree in English literature and spent most of her career as a freelance information analyst. Her poems have appeared in literary magazines in Israel and abroad. She is currently President of the Israeli English-language poetry society, Voices Israel.

Latham, Tamara Beryl is a retired Research and Development chemist who is originally from Brisbane, Australia, but currently resides in Virginia. Tamara was the Forum Moderator for Metric Poetry on the Moontown Cafe.com internet site. Her work has appeared in numerous publications, anthologies and literary reviews.

LeKane, Shari Jo lives in St. Louis, Missouri. She writes poetry, prose and articles, and specializes in literary criticism, creative writing, Spanish Language and culture, business and community development, educational and leadership development, nonprofit matters, and disability and elderly care and advocacy. She has a B.A. in English and Spanish, an M.A. in Spanish from Saint Louis University in Madrid and St. Louis, and additional certifications. She teaches Spanish at a college in St. Louis, and Creative Writing and Poetry. Shari's poetry has been published in literary magazines worldwide.

Lukey, Benjamin Daniel lives in Monroe, North Carolina. He teaches high school English classes whenever he is not fishing or writing poetry. Read more of his poems at hellopoetry.com/bdlukey.

Magdalen, Daniel is a doctoral student in the Faculty of Letters at the University of Bucharest, in Romania.

Maibach, Michael Charles began writing poems at age 9. Since then, he has continued writing poems and sharing them with friends. His career has involved global business diplomacy. He is a native of Peoria, Illinois. Today Michael resides in Old Town Alexandria, Virginia. His poems can be viewed at MaibachPoems.us

Mantyk, Evan teaches history and literature in the Hudson Valley region of New York. He is president of The Society of Classical Poets, as well as chief editor of its website and Journal. His most recent book of poetry, *Heroes of the East and West*, was published in 2020.

McGrath, Reid lives and writes in the Hudson Valley region of New York. His most recent book of poetry, *Juvenalia*, was published by Kelsay Books in 2019.

Miller, Michael received his Master's in English from San Francisco State University from the Creative Writing Department. He was a finalist in the 2020 San Francisco Writers Conference Fiction Contest. Living in Seattle, he is recently retired from a career as a software engineer and participates in writing workshops at Richard Hugo House.

Moe, Rita is the author of two poetry chapbooks, *Sins & Disciplines* and *Findley Place; A Street, a Ballpark, a Neighborhood*. Now retired from an investment firm in Minneapolis, she lives in Roseville, Minnesota.

Mootsey, Bethany is a stay-at-home mom and foster mom living in Clearwater, Florida. She is a Covenant College graduate with publications in "Church Educator."

Murel, Jake is a PhD Candidate in Boston, MA.

Palmer, Brian is managing editor of the literary journal, *THINK*. He earned his MFA in Creative Writing-Poetry Concentration at Western Colorado University. He lives in Grand Junction, Colorado.

Palmer, Sasha A. is a Russian-born writer and translator, who currently lives in Maryland. Sasha is the recipient of international awards in poetry and translation.

Pain, Norma was born in Liverpool, England and now lives in Parksville, British Columbia, Canada. Thirty of Norma's poems were published by Dana Literary Society, between 2004 and 2007 and she was twice nominated for the Pushcart Prize by that same on-line poetry site. She self-published a book of rhyme in 2000 called *Bulging Assets*.

Parson, Jon, has been a trial lawyer in California for over 40 years helping small businesses and individuals navigate an increasingly difficult environment.

Payne, Johnny is a native Kentuckian. He directs the MFA in Creative Writing at Mount Saint Mary's University, Los Angeles. His books of published poetry are *Heaven of Ashes* and *Vassal*.

Peterson, Roy E. is an author, former diplomat, and retired U.S. Army Military Intelligence and Russian Foreign Area Officer who currently resides in Texas.

Rieger, K. Irene is Associate Professor of English at Bluefield University in Bluefield, Virginia. A Martha's Vineyard Institute of Creative Writing Fellow, she is the First Place winner of the 88th Annual Writer's Digest Writing Competition in Rhyming Poetry.

Rizley, Martin grew up in Oklahoma and in Texas, and has served in pastoral ministry both in the United States and in Europe. He is currently serving as the pastor of a small evangelical church in the city of Málaga on the southern coast of Spain.

Robin, Damian lives in England, where he works as a copyeditor and proofreader. He lives with his wife and two of their three adult children. He won Second Place in the Society's 2014 Poetry Competition.

Rogers, Phil S. is a sixth generation Vermonter, age 72, now retired and living in Texas. He served in the U.S. Air Force and had a career in real estate and banking. He previously published *Everlasting Glory*, a historical work.

Rubstein, Alex is an twelfth-grade student home-schooled in Canton Aargau, Switzerland.

Sale, James is a worldwide thought leader on motivation. He has had four books on the topic published by Routledge, and over seven hundred management consultants in fifteen countries use his products. James is also a feature writer on culture for *The Epoch Times*. He has written poetry for over fifty years and has had nine collections published. He won First Prize in the Society's 2017 Competition. His next collection, *The English Cantos Volume 1: HellWard*, is due shortly. For more on this, go to EnglishCantos.home.blog. He can be contacted at james@motivationalmaps.com

Salemi, Joseph S. has published five books of poetry, and his poems, translations, and scholarly articles have appeared in over one hundred publications worldwide. He is the editor of the literary magazine *Trinacria*. He teaches in the Department of Humanities at New York University and in the Department of Classical Languages at Hunter College.

Sarangi, Satyananda, an electrical engineering alumnus of Indira Gandhi Institute of Technology, is a young poet and editor who enjoys reading Longfellow, Shelley, Coleridge, Yeats, Blake, and many others. His works have been widely published in India, Germany, and the United States, among other countries. Currently, he resides in Odisha, India.

Sedia, Adam (b. 1984) lives in his native Northwest where he practices law as a civil and appellate litigator. He is also a composer, and his musical works may be heard on his YouTube channel.

Smagacz, Geoffrey writes from South Carolina and Mexico. A collection of his fiction, titled *A Waste of Shame and Other Sad Tales of the Appalachian Foothills* (Wiseblood Books, 2013), won the 2014 Independent Publisher gold medal for Best Mid-Atlantic Regional Fiction.

Stock, Beverly lives in St. Louis, Missouri. Look for more of her work on her website: BeverlyStockPoetry.com

Stone, Mark F. grew up near Seattle, Washington. After graduating from Brandeis University and Stanford Law School, he worked as an attorney for the U.S. Air Force for thirty-three years. He served for eleven years as an active duty Air Force JAG attorney. He then served twenty-two years as an Air Force civilian attorney (while serving part time in the Air Force Reserves as a JAG attorney). He lives in central Ohio.

Strano, Ellie is a ninth-grade student homeschooled in Lexington, MA.

Tessitore, Joe is a retired New York City resident and poet.

Thompson, Sean is a medical student from the United Kingdom.

Tweedie, James A. is a retired pastor living in Long Beach, Washington. He has written and self-published four novels and a collection of short stories.

Villanueva, Angel L. is a religious man who resides in Massachusetts, enjoying a simple life.

Wasem, Adam is a writer living in Chicago.

Watt, David is a writer from Canberra, the "Bush Capital" of Australia. When not working for IP (Intellectual Property) Australia, he finds time to appreciate the intrinsic beauty of traditional rhyming poetry. He was the First Place winner in the Friends of Falun Gong Poetry Contest 2018.

Whippman, David is a British poet, now retired after a career in healthcare. Over the years he's had quite a few poems, articles, and short stories published in various magazines.

Willis, Lionel was born in Toronto in 1932. He has been a mosaic designer, portrait painter, watercolorist, biological illustrator, field entomologist and professor of English Literature as well as a poet. His verse has appeared in two books, *The Dreamstone and Other Rhymes* (The Plowman, 2003) and *Heartscape, a Book of Bucolic Verse* (EIDOLON, 2019).

Winick, Russel recently started writing poetry at nearly age 65, after ending a long legal career. He resides in Naperville, Illinois.

Wise, Bruce Dale is a poet living in Texas who often writes under anagrammatic heteronyms. He won First Prize in the Society of Classical Poets' 2014 Competition.

Wood, Arthur L. is a poet from Winchester, United Kingdom. He has published two collections, *Poems for Susan* (2020) and *Scarlet Land* (2021). He runs his own YouTube channel "Poetry from the Shires" where he shares classic and original verse. His poetry collections is available at ko-fi.com/arthurlwood/shop. Find him on Twitter: @ArthurLWood

Woodruff, Julian D. was a teacher, orchestral musician, and librarian. He served for several years as librarian at the Crocker Art Museum in Sacramento, California. He now resides in the area of Rochester, New York, where he writes poetry and fiction, much of it for children.

Yapko, Brian is a lawyer who also writes poetry. He lives in Santa Fe, New Mexico.

Yee, Hannah is a ninth-grade student homeschooled in Massachusetts.

CLASSICAL POETS PUBLISHING

© 2022 — SOCIETY OF CLASSICAL POETS
ALL RIGHTS RESERVED

www.ingramcontent.com/pod-product-compliance
Lightning Source LLC
Chambersburg PA
CBHW041323110526
44592CB00021B/2801